Renewing Your Mind

Mona Johnian

BRIDGE PUBLISHING, INC.
South Plainfield, NJ 07080

Unless otherwise indicated all Scripture
has been quoted from the *King James
Version* of the Bible.

Renewing Your Mind
ISBN 0-88270-662-4
Library of Congress # 93-070312
Copyright © 1993 by Mona Johnian

Published by:
Bridge Publishing Inc.
2500 Hamilton Blvd.
South Plainfield, NJ 07080

Contents

Preface

"I saw differently,
I thought differently,
I felt differently."

Steven Covey
Seven Habits of Effective People

This is the sequence to a renewed self. You will never "feel" the way you want until you "think" the way you should.

This book is written to help you "see" in yourself a new possibility.

—Mona Johnian

1

Admitting Your Need

A few years ago, a series of circumstances forced us to move on short notice. Limited finances and inflation compelled us to take a drab, neglected house. Even on the brightest days, we had to turn on several lamps just to have minimal light.

I have never liked dimly lighted houses. I love light and want things to look fresh and clean. Consequently, I disliked living in the "Dark Hole," as we called it. I could hardly wait to move out.

But the "Dark Hole" is where I live today, as owner. What happened? One day I was walking in a furniture store, and my eyes fell upon a design an interior decorator had arranged. It looked similar to my fireplace and was so beautiful that I caught an instant vision of how to bring my own house alive!

With one vision and one new thought, light came into our home and changed it into a lovely, pleasant place to enjoy life.

That is the power of one thought and its ability to renew your drab, dark way of looking at yourself. One new way of seeing your possibilities can flood you with light and hope. I know because it happened not only to my house, but to my emotions.

Change and renewal are a daily possibility!

I am not talking about an instantaneous mind transplant. I am not even suggesting that you will wake up tomorrow morning in a tropical paradise. What I am talking about is much more substantial than vending machine solutions.

When I say you can *renew* your mind, I am referring to the same process through which we took our dark house. That is exactly what the word renew means—"to renovate."

This book is going to help you renovate the place where your thoughts live! Your mind, body, and spirit—all three are the dwelling place of your thoughts, for good or bad.

Thoughts are words waiting to be expressed. Good thoughts and good words are the greatest tools you possess for carving out your place in life. I cannot say enough about the value of words.

Years ago, as I was growing up in the midst of a ten-member family, my father often used a quaint word we children assumed he had fabricated out of his colorful vocabulary. Whenever one of us mentioned the qualities of a new boy or girlfriend we were interested in, my father would respond, "Yes, but does he have the *spondulas*?"

As we grew into adulthood and our father rested from his labors, we forgot his animated expression. That word, which we never understood, was lost to us completely. Then one day last spring, my brother went to England for a tour of Christian businessmen's meetings. During a conversation with an aging Englishman, the gentleman used the word *spondulas!*

"What does that word mean?" my brother eagerly inquired. "My father often used it when we were children, but we never thought it really meant anything."

"Oh, yes," the Englishman responded, "spondulas is an old word we use for money." Of course! Our father was a successful businessman. Completely intolerant of laziness, he believed in hard work. A young man who had no spondulas must be lacking in "spunk" and was no fit prospect for his daughters.

When my brother told me about rediscovering that special word from childhood, it was like a momentary visit with our wonderful father. A little part of him, that lighter side, reappeared for a brief moment.

Words are the language of our heart. They cause us to be able to plant ourselves in each other's life for good or negative results. If our word-plantings are good, we reap beautiful relationships and harmonious societies. If our thoughts are destructive, we pull apart from ourselves, each other, and society.

Unfortunately, most of us need renovation. The bulk of our words are defenses, attacks, and reactions that require daily change and renewal. Just as we renovated our home from dark depression, it is possible to re-do a mental make-up and become vibrant—as much as you are willing.

You can be as happy, as excited, and as hopeful as you will. I say "as you will" because it is up to you to make the changes. Just as it was up to my husband and me to clean, paint, strip, sand, carpet, and refurnish the "Dark Hole," it is up to you to renovate your way of looking at your circumstances.

God says, "Be constantly renewed in the spirit of your mind—having a fresh mental and spiritual attitude" (Ephesians 4:23, *Amplified*). Now, if for some reason you do not believe in God or His power to help with mental and emotional problems, then I encourage you to give His method a chance. You have tried everything else. Why not try His way?

For years I tried psychology books, tranquilizers, psychiatrists, the arts, and intellectual pursuits, but I remained an emotional wreck. I even vacillated from spectator to participant in church activities. I was a believer in Christ and a Bible reader. I loved God. But I needed mental renovation.

That is when I decided to go back to my Manufacturer and see what He could do. I made the decision to "give it all I had." I would not dabble but plunge, head first, right into the middle of "mental and spiritual" renewal.

Unbelieving people need mental renovation; believing people need mental restoration. If they did not, then why would the apostle Paul write to the Church saying, "Be renewed in the spirit of your mind"?

If you are miserable, if you are desperate, and if you see life passing you by, then why not come with me to visit the Manufacturer, follow His instructions, and see what can happen?

Houses come and go, but minds and lives are too precious not to renovate to maximum potential.

Admit Your Need

Do you want to be happy? You can be, but it is going to take change—a lot of change, according to your original design.

This brings us to point one of a potent prescription I found in the book of Ephesians that says: " ...rejecting all falsity" (Ephesians 4:25, *Amplified*).

The King James translation says, "putting away lying." All lying hurts, but lying to yourself will hurt you most of all. No change or improvement has ever been experienced unless first preceded by honesty.

If you cannot admit that you need help, then help will never come. If, on the other hand, you can say to yourself that it is you—not your neighbor—who needs to change, then you are already on your way to recovering happiness.

Say it out loud: "I have faults."

"I need to change my way of thinking and acting."

"I can change my ways with the help of God, and I will!"

It didn't hurt all that badly, did it? The sky didn't fall in. The world didn't stop turning. You admitted to your own fallibility, and everything around you is still intact.

Good!

You have just discovered a great "release valve" guaranteed to move a ton of pressure off your life any time you will use it.

Confess Your Faults

God calls this aspect of mental renewal "confessing your faults" in His James 5:16 prescription. Confession

5

begins with admission. You will always find pressure instantaneously released from your mind as you *admit to your own faults.* Being honest with yourself and with others is an essential ingredient to sound, stable emotions. It is always step one to effective renovation.

A woman came up to me one evening and mentioned a family we both knew. "I hate that family!" she said bluntly just as we were getting ready to enter into worship. I rushed up to the front of the auditorium a bit stunned by her anger and joined my husband, Paul, in some music. The service that evening had a beautiful presence of peace, and my mind wandered over to this woman several times.

When the evening concluded and everyone was milling toward the exit, this same woman came up to me and said, "Excuse me for a minute. I just want you to know I was wrong in what I said about that family—I apologize." You see, she was confessing her own faults and relieving the pressure of anger from her emotions. The Holy Spirit convinced her of her wrong attitude. She admitted to herself and confessed it to God—then she wanted me to know about the correction.

In other words, she washed herself clean of that entire situation. She experienced no self-crucifixion and no excessive penance—just a clean admission of guilt and she was liberated. Is it difficult for you to admit to your faults? Do you often try to justify or rationalize your mistakes?

IRRITABILITY

Are you irritable in your home or at your job because of "other" people? If so, let's enter into a little housecleaning for a minute.

You are what you are because you choose to be that way. This may be painful to accept, but it is true. Our temperament is ours by choice. We lack control over many things in life, but our temperament or nature is not one of them. We can be in mental and moral character exactly what we desire to be.

If you are an irritable, high-strung person, then that is the nature you choose. "Oh," you may say, "but I have this health condition." The Holy Spirit in you is able to control the mind of even the physically infirm. Rise up in your spirit and take authority over unruly emotions that continue to pour grime into your life and relationships!

When your thoughts begin to run off in the direction of anger, simply put the reins on them just the way you would harness a new pony: "Whoa there!"

IMMORALITY

Have you ever heard unfaithful husbands or wives say, "I was driven to it." They were. But what they usually fail to admit is that *they were the driver!*

"I was driven to immorality by loneliness—or my cruel husband—or my frigid wife."

No, you are unfaithful because of your own weakness toward immorality. Admit to the truth, and you will have dealt the problem a deadly blow.

Admit it to yourself, and confess it to God.

Immorality is not the only outlet for lonely, abused, and denied people. Be honest with yourself. If this is one of your problems, ask God to show you a more constructive way of releasing pent-up emotions.

7

Domineering

Another problem area we find in human nature, which most of us have a hard time admitting, is the desire to dominate. Naturally speaking, we human beings love to control! Trying to control other people is one of the most frustrating things in the world because we love to control equally as much as we hate being dominated!

Control and domination are the instigators of all relationship struggles. Nations try it, and individuals try it, but no one is ever really successful. We all hate dictatorship.

Trying to dominate those around you creates great mental strain. Perhaps you have consoled yourself with the idea that life has awarded you this great burden. You just naturally know better than anyone else. Don't you believe it! That is one of those lies from which the Ephesian prescription (Ephesians 4:23) is trying to cure you. Human beings are domineering, controlling, and dictatorial by choice. In our everyday relationships, we call this condition being "bossy." Bossy people need to be honest. No one person knows better than anyone else on all subjects.

God recently taught me a beautiful lesson on this point. He said quite simply, "Much stress in life is caused by people failing to know their place."

The colonel is not in command of the pickle factory. The lawyer is not in charge of the hospital. The doctor is not the big shot of the restaurant. The musician will not prevent worldwide starvation, and the "liberated gender" will not automatically know more than the President.

People who try to control all situations are playing God. It is far less stressful to be honest and admit that we are only human beings with one specialty and a few minor areas of contribution.

The day I got the courage to say, "I am wrong," was one of the best days of my life. "I don't know" was something I could never admit. I always felt compelled to produce the answer. Now that I have admitted to my own limitations, I feel perfectly free to say, "I'm sorry, I don't have the answer."

What music, not only to my ears but to those who live and work with me. They love working with a fallible human being. It helps other people to hear you say, "I'm wrong," "I'm sorry," or "It was my mistake." They love it. That way they feel free to admit their own weaknesses as well.

One day my husband Paul and I disagreed about the way to handle a situation. I started upstairs where Paul was studying, and with each step I gained steam! As I reached the top, Paul called out, "Mona, do whatever you like about the situation. That is more your department than mine."

Do you know what I did? I immediately deflated into a speechless dish of jelly. Just when I was all set to explode like dynamite, I suddenly had nothing to say. Paul had gotten over into my department. He realized it, admitted it, and that ended it. Thank God peace was restored, and harmony began to produce its sweet music.

The Ephesian prescription says, "Renew your mind, put away falsehoods." Be honest with yourself and with others.

Admit—Abandon

Remember, *admitting* to your faults is not the same as *accepting* them. Some people take pride in recounting their orneriness. They wear faults like a badge of honor. When God says to admit or "confess your faults," He means to do so with the intention of changing.

To admit your faults and the need to change is one thing; but confession will not, in fact, change you unless you live up to your confession. Admitting your faults and then abandoning them entirely is the only step to a better way of living.

Admit—abandon.

Are you ready to be renovated? Sanded? Blasted? Solvents used on you? Stripped? Painted? Varnished? Recovered? Are you ready for a complete internal overhaul? Then let's go to the great internal physician and begin the rejuvenating process.

Pin this on your mirror and pray it daily: "Lord, I admit to myself and confess to You that I need changing. There are miserable areas of my life for which I have blamed other people. But now I understand that I am the one who is responsible. I ask You to forgive me for my own sins. (Name them if they are obvious. Don't worry if you can't identify your problem areas at the moment, and don't try to dig up more than God shows you today.) I ask You now, Lord Jesus, to come into my mind and completely renew my way of thinking. I surrender to Your total mental, emotional, physical, and spiritual renovation."

Now, get up and go find someone with whom to share your new decision. Call someone on the phone—

just tell it. It is never too late to be renewed. Old houses are the most beautiful once they have undergone loving reconstruction.

Remember, God does not see you as the broken or abusive person you may have become. He sees what He created in the beginning and what you can become once again under His personal refinement.

Admitting to your own need to change is the first step in your quest for a new and better way of thinking.

2

Forgiveness

We are talking about renewing your mind, renovation, changing your way of thinking, improving the quality of your life through a new way of coping with yourself, other people, and situations.

In the last chapter, I talked about our buying a neglected house and turning it into something attractive. Another aspect of that purchase will help bring you to a second important step toward good mental health.

After Paul and I decided to purchase the "Dark Hole," we contacted a long time "friend" to start the procedures. And a procedure is just what he initiated: He proceeded to squeeze every dime out of us he possibly could.

Our friend, someone we trusted to be fair, had suddenly turned into a man without moral conscience. Whatever the law allowed, he did.

It did not take long for me to build up a good case of righteous indignation against his covetous attitude. I found myself imagining all I was going to say and do when we signed those final papers. I meant to get our friend as well as the greedy owner. "I'll show them!" I said to myself.

But God paid me several calls and reversed my decision. Instead of cursing them with intent to destroy, I blessed them with hunger and thirst to know Jesus.

It was a long, drawn-out process where I had the opportunity to resist the "I'll show them!" urge many times. I did resist, however, based on my personal knowledge of what unforgiveness had done to me in the past—emotionally as well as physically. I knew I could not afford such luxury a second time.

I had been learning about forgiveness and resentment all of my life. Being of sensitive temperament, I was often cut to the bone by situations Paul or someone else hardly noticed. Strangely enough, I had a low tolerance for other people who overreacted as I often did. Let me give you an example.

ANGER • DEPRESSION • UNFORGIVENESS

One evening, I was getting ready to speak when a girl came up to me with a proposal she thought was good. Unfortunately, it was very bad, and I had to say "no."

Well, that girl came and planted herself in the front row of the auditorium and sat there crying and looking like a beaten dog the entire time I was speaking. When you discover I was speaking about our "loving Father," you will see the emotional tangle I felt inside. There I stood, all smiles, while the evidence before me beamed out my obvious cruelty.

When that meeting was over, I wanted to yank that young woman out of her chair and spank her like the spoiled brat she was! I was literally fuming—so much so that I went to the back of the room to try and calm down. But the longer I sat there, the more nervous I felt. Finally, an old familiar band began to tighten around my neck, and I felt as though I were choking. I knew then that nerves had come in for the kill.

"Hold it!" I said in my mind. "This is all blown out of proportion. Father, help me to get control of myself. Show me what to do."

Then the Lord gave me another Ephesian prescription: "Be angry and sin not ... " (4:26).

Yes, I was angry. And anger, undealt with, either turns on you or the other person. If it turns inward, you become *depressed*; if anger turns outward, it becomes *unforgiveness*.

Depression and unforgiveness are the twin daughters of anger. And you are the victim when either one of them moves into your mental compartment.

"Okay, Lord, I see it now. I am angry at Bridget. But I don't want to be. What should I do?" In my present emotional state, I could not think of the appropriate action. I only knew I wanted to be free from this nervous attack.

"Forgive her!" the Lord said. "If you want release, forgive her for what she did."

"But, Lord, she's such a big baby!"

"That's right. Forgive her. Forgive her for being a big baby."

"Lord, I forgive Bridget for what she did, and I ask You to bless her," I prayed. The very moment the word

15

"forgive" came out of my mouth, I felt a pressure release in my chest as real as letting air out of a tire. I relaxed; I stopped shaking; perspective came back into my mind; and I remembered that Bridget always cries when she does not get her way. Yet, she has a dozen other positive qualities that outweigh her few negative ones.

You may have been carrying around old grudges, old wounds, or old conversations that had a simple beginning, like the one I related. I know several young women today who spend valuable time on such trivia. Every word spoken to them is like a can placed in a compactor—it comes out completely distorted.

Some of you, on the other hand, may be carrying around real, bonafide situations that merit your anger: That person may deserve your wrath. That situation might even win you some easy money in court. Humanly speaking, you may have every right to hate several people for what they have done to you. But how much is vengeance worth to you?

VENGEANCE

Is paying back someone worth your emotional health? Is it worth your physical health? Is it worth your peace of mind? Would you really rather hate than be happy? Beyond your physical and emotional health, is revenge worth your peace with God? The Lord said that He forgives only those who forgive. (See Matthew 18:35.)

It is amazing how many people think God hates "that person" as much as they do. They honestly believe that they and God are two against the world! I had a young married woman say to me, "I hate my husband as much as I can get away with and still get into heaven!"

But my Book for Living, the Bible, says, "Whoever despises, despises not man but God" (1 Thessalonians 4:8). God is not a partner with any person's hatred or unforgiveness.

What does the Ephesian prescription say? "Be angry and sin not." How can I sin when I am angry? By failing to forgive.

When gas is heated, the molecules go bouncing madly in every direction. Unless there is a release valve, it will soon cause a destructive explosion. Imagine a fire set under a gas truck. The same is true when we are wounded. The wound is a flame set under our nervous system. It may be one word or a literal physical attack. But unless we extinguish the fire quickly, pressure will build up inside us, and we will either explode onto the other person or keep it within and go into depression.

How can we release internal pressure and keep it from causing real or imagined wounds? Simple. *Forgive people!* It may not be easy, but it is simple: "I forgive them." Why should you forgive them?

- Because God requires it.
- Because your nerves need it.
- Because your body demands it.
- And ... because you are not perfect either!

Unforgiveness is demanding *perfection* out of other people—a level of conduct that you, yourself, cannot attain. Sometimes they may be wrong. Sometimes you may be wrong. Sometimes you may both be off target. Quite often the situation is just that—a story with two sides.

Let me give you my classic example of an argument between two "dead right" persons thoroughly convinced of their own positions. I call it, "The case of Hado, Huto, Hodo."

One evening, my husband and I were driving along in a great mood, when Paul said, "You know, I was just thinking of that beautiful time we had a few months ago at Mrs. Huto's house. It was just a beautiful move of God, wasn't it?"

"Yes, it was," I responded, "but the name is Hado."

"No, it was Huto."

"Hado."

"You're wrong, it was Huto."

"No, Paul. If you want to erroneously believe the woman's name was Huto, go ahead, but I know it is Hado."

"Huto!"

"Hado!"

I settled back in the most smug certainty possible and said to myself, "He has never had the ear for words that I do!" A few weeks later we were at a convention, and a woman came up to us smiling and said, "Paul and Mona! What a thrill to see you. Remember me? A few months ago we met at the home of Mrs. Hodo."

What a good laugh Paul and I had after the woman left us. We had both been so absolute in our position, but they both turned out absolutely wrong. And so it is. Having to be "dead right" all the time is deadly. It destroys relationships. Is it too great a sacrifice to allow others their opinion and then, when they are wrong, forgive them? Forgiveness is a law of health that releases the pressure of daily anger. If we ignore it, we explode. If we obey it, we find the secret to renewal.

Right now, begin a new way of coping with the tongue and actions of other people. I am going to ask you to forgive that person.

Sit down with a paper and pencil and list every person who has hurt you—small and great. Then bring them one by one to the Lord, saying, "Father, I forgive (call the name), and I ask You to bless their life abundantly."

Then every time they come to your mind, instead of grinding, speak a quick blessing on them. "Bless so and so, Father." Do it until you have complete inner release from the situation. Forgiveness is the key to coping with other people's violations and mistakes.

But what about your own faults? Do you find it difficult to allow yourself the same tolerance you allow other people? Are you like a traffic officer who always puts his own name on the ticket? Are you the accused who must always stand trial—guilty, with no hope of pardon? If you can extend forgiveness to every other person besides yourself, then I want to talk to you for a moment.

FORGIVING YOURSELF

People have a very sensitive area of their lives involving self-forgiveness. I know I speak for millions when I say that I have robbed my life of many good years because I felt compelled to bring each of my painful mistakes into my mind's laboratory for thorough and frequent examination. I have scrutinized the "why's" and dissected the "if only's." I have colonized projected failures and incubated them into overpopulated regions. No one hates our mistakes as much as we do. No one finds it as difficult to forgive us as we do to forgive ourselves.

Our minds are in great need of reform on this matter of self-forgiveness. The ability to forgive yourself cannot happen until you get a healthy and realistic view of your past. People who are filled with *regrets* never find the fountain of forgiveness.

Did you ever see the old Jimmy Stewart movie where he was facing bankruptcy and decided to commit suicide so his family could have his life insurance benefits? Just as he was about to jump from an icy bridge, an angel appeared and began to reason with him. "I wish I had never been born," the distraught man contended. Then the angel proceeded to show him how different the world would have been if, in fact, he had not been born. (I wish they still made good movies like that.)

Using this premise, I began to think about my own hateful past. Taking those scenes I wanted most to change, I began to see that rather than erasing the existence of those people and events from my life, I would rather be forgiven.

Why don't you stop for a moment and try the same experiment? For example, let's say you have suffered a divorce. That is a regret in your past. You may have great cause to blame yourself. You have probably wished you had never married.

In reality, do you really wish your children were not born or that you had never met all the people your life has touched through your marriage relationship? Was it really a total, miserable loss?

Some people hate their childhood. They find it difficult to forgive their parents. I used to hate working in the cotton fields of Alabama! We were not poor, but my father believed in hard work. When my sister and I were ten and twelve years old, we were given three acres of cotton to plant and harvest. All proceeds were ours to put into our own bank accounts. I hated the work, but I learned many good lessons from that responsibility. Years later, I am still grateful for the wonderful parents God gave me to prepare for greater responsibilities as an adult.

Some people have committed crimes in their past. But once their minds have been renewed, they have taken their ugly scars and won starring roles as examples of rehabilitation. Thousands need to know that good can come out of disaster.

One day I said, "Lord, surely my sins have no redemptive value!"

He said, "Even your sins can work for you, once you have forgiven yourself and turned them over to me."

"How, Lord?" I inquired.

"Your heart, not your sin, caused your problems," the Lord showed me. "When you commit sins, you are simply exposing what you have hidden deep inside your inner self."

One evening I lost my temper with an elderly woman in a restaurant. "You were wrong, Mona," Paul said.

"I was right!" I contended.

"Wrong!"

"Right!"

"Would you want Jesus to be sitting in the next booth?"

"Wrong!"

With the admission of guilt, I began to feel condemned. I was shocked at my ugly display. All evening and into the next day I felt terrible. Finally, the Lord began to bring renewal into my mind.

"Don't be overwhelmed by your conduct, Mona," He encouraged me. "I already knew you had that potential down in your heart; you are the only one who thought you were perfect."

I meet people who would like to have a personal relationship with God, but they do not feel qualified because of their past mistakes. Then I meet others who started out with God, but quit once they realized they were not as perfect as He. "I just can't measure up," they say in surrender.

Somewhere in the ego of our secret imagination, we human beings have told ourselves that we could be perfect. Therefore, when we fail—especially when we fail God—we simply cannot find the justification to go on. We know that He knows the truth. *We are not perfect.* But we cannot cope with being found out, so we cop-out. Are you having difficulty forgiving yourself because you live with regrets and embarrassing reminders of past blunders? Then let me give you some steps I have taken:

1. Be realistic about your past. Thoughts exaggerate with time. Any situation always seems better or worse than it actually was when you view it in retrospect.

If you cannot see any good in your past, then you have an unrealistic view. Your mind has taken one portion of your life and blown it out of proportion in regard to all other experiences.

On the other hand, fantasizing that your past was perfect will rob you of today with its ups and downs. You were never perfect, and neither were your circumstances. Get a balanced view of the past. It contains both good and bad, success and failure.

As long as you live, you will need to be forgiven by God and other people. And because you are a fallible human being, you will need to forgive yourself. You may have sung a wrong note, or you may have hurt someone beyond repair. It is natural to condemn yourself.

But you do not have to be imprisoned by regrets and self-condemnation over your past mistakes. Your past has no prison bars on it—only your attitude toward it has any real power. Your attitude is the *hope* or the *handicap* that makes your past a plus or minus in your life today.

Most people need to hold a massive funeral service—literally. At that ceremony they need to bury once and for all their griefs, grievances, mistakes, sins, dead relationships, and old wounds. They need to bury those hurts, not out of fear, but by conscious choice. Instead of repressing the pain and pretending it did not happen, they need to capture those nagging thoughts that have become anxieties and seal their fate once and for all. By the will a person can annihilate dead issues of the past.

2. Admit that you can never change the past. Forget it! Some of you need to grasp this reality. You may bury the past, but you can *never* change it. You may understand the past, but you can never change it. In fact, it will help you now to say out loud, "I cannot change the past."

Will you also take the next step and confess, "I will stop trying to change the past," and then stop trying? Grieving over past mistakes and trying to change them is not a noble pursuit. It sounds so holy and humble to show the world that you are grieving over your sins and errors. But the truth is, living in a state of regret and self-condemnation is unholy and self-centered.

You will not find one Scripture where God instructed someone to change the past. Jacob was a young man who stole his brother's spiritual family blessing as well as the family's choice property. Later in life, he repented of his conduct and even restored material wealth to his brother. But Jacob did not spend his life in regret. Neither did God tell him to try and undo his violation. *Repentance* and *forgiveness* was God's solution for Jacob. Then God blessed him with twelve fine sons and national prominence.

Even God himself did not try to undo the past. When His first man and woman failed, God did not wring His hands saying, "If only ... tell me one more time how it happened!... Let's take it step by step ... was anyone else listening? What did they think?"

A thousand times, no! Instead of regrets, God mapped out a plan to *overcome* the past through repentance and forgiveness.

If you will ever become a whole person, you must live in a state of continual repentance and forgiveness. That forgiveness must include your own violations as well as the unlawful acts of others against you.

You must learn to view yourself with the same tolerance as God does when He looks at you. If you could have achieved perfection, then Jesus would not have had to die. The very fact that He was crucified tells you and me that we have the right to make and overcome our mistakes.

Stop daydreaming about natural perfection! Don't be shocked when your immature reactions stick up their ugly heads. While your conduct may grieve God, it will never shock Him. You are fallible. As long as you live you will make mistakes, but you are not chained to those errors unless you refuse to forgive.

Say, "Father, in Jesus' Name, I confess that I hold unforgiveness against myself. I do not like myself when I am not perfect. I hate myself whenever I make mistakes and blunders. I ask You to forgive and remove this self-hatred from me. And I thank You that You created me with a good design and purpose. I will no longer grind over my past failures but ask instead that You turn them into good for me and for Your work in the lives of other hurting people. Thank You for forgiving my mistakes, Father. Now, I forgive myself."

We counseled with a distraught young mother one evening for about two hours. We were not far into the prayer ministry we use in helping people walk into the freedom and love of God, when the young woman suddenly jumped up and beat her fists against the desk. "Oh, no," she cried out.

Do you know what she found impossible? My husband asked her to say, "I forgive myself."

Her life painted a familiar portrait of today's generation. She had been on a drug, alcohol, sex, cult, and occult merry-go-round, and now her shattered mind was searching for peace. Yes, she was a committed Christian and faithful in the church. From all appearance, she was playing it by the rules now; but her mind was in desperate need of renewal. She needed a complete renovation of the way she viewed herself—past, present, and future.

Nobody is a zero. Yet almost every person who finds his or her way to a counseling room feels like a failure. How terribly wounded the human race has become.

That young mother carried such self-hatred and self-rejection that we literally had to walk through her despised past and encourage her at each check point to say, "I forgive myself." But what a beautiful restoration she experienced once she accepted forgiveness from God and toward herself!

Are you willing to forgive yourself? Are you willing to face any mistakes you have been trying to hide or change through self-condemnation and render them harmless—never again to be resurrected? If so, then here is what you do: List on a piece of paper the things about yourself that you have been unable to forgive. For example:

<u>My Past</u>

- My mother.
- My father.
- My childhood.
- My business failure.
- My marriage failure.
- God.

My Body

- I hate the way I look.
- I hate my size.
- I hate my physical impairment.
- I hate my parents for my physical condition.

My Attitude

- I am filled with self-hatred.
- I have a fear of rejection.
- I am filled with bitterness and anger.
- I want to destroy myself.
- I wish I were dead.
- I would like to see some people I know die.
- I am hostile and would like to hurt some body the way I have been hurt

Take each one of these feelings and deal with it, once and for all. Say out loud, "Father God, I confess to You that I feel _____. I ask You to forgive me, and I receive my forgiveness in Jesus' name. I forgive myself."

Complete your list, tear it up, and throw it away. Then when those old negative, accusing thoughts begin to drift back into your mind, simply say, "No! You do not occupy my life; you will not occupy my mind. I am free, and I am forgiven!"

When a new mistake comes to the surface, deal with it quickly and permanently in the same manner: Take the error to God, confess your guilt, and forgive yourself. You will never be perfect in all your decisions, but you are perfectly acceptable to God as long as you continue in forgiveness.

3

Guilt

We are going to start this chapter on mental renewal with an experiment. I am going to say a word, then I want you to speak the first thing that comes into your mind.

Ready? Here goes ....

"Guilty!"

Be perfectly honest. How many of you said, "That's me!" when I said the word "guilty"?

I have used this experiment many times with an audience, and a large percentage invariably raise their hands in admission of their guilt feelings. That is what we are going to be dealing with in this chapter—guilt feelings, real and false.

Every person begins a relationship with guilt as a child. We first experience those "yucky" feelings as a result of telling "little white lies," reading "dirty books," or engaging in sexual investigation with a buddy who comes over to play. Even before our parents suspected and warned us of a specific violation, a signal went off inside us that said we had stepped from the path of innocence to guilt.

When I was only four years old, we lived beside a family whose daughters had beautiful doll clothes. Thinking I just had to have one such article, I deftly tucked a little dress underneath my shirt and went skipping home. But my joy was cut short when I tried to explain to my mother how I had found the doll dress outside. Even in the middle of my juvenile fabrication guilt began to rob my pleasure.

Real guilt is uncomfortable at any age, although some people believe it would not exist if society would relax its imposing standards. Their philosophy is simply to erase the book and remove the reality.

One of our friends took this position one evening during a lively discussion on the subject. "Guilt feelings are the result of outdated expressions, such as 'wrong,' 'immoral,' and 'evil,'" he contended. "Look at the nations that are sexually liberated and see how much better it works when people stop trying to make other people feel guilty."

"In other words," I rebutted, "would there be no more disease if we would simply wipe out all doctors and hospitals?"

This popular concept states that rules create violations. But let's take that equation a step further: If rules create violations and God's Word creates guilt, then doctors must create sickness, banks create robbers, traffic signals create accidents, the atmosphere creates pollution, and the hungry create starvation.

Guilt is real! It would exist if every rule book throughout society were burned and forgotten. We live in a world of law and order. We fly planes by its rules, eat according to its dictates, and light our homes at night by its principles. Real guilt feelings are the result of real violations of real existing laws, whether or not they are written with ink and paper.

The feeling of guilt resulting from wrongdoing—stated in God's laws for society—is known as real guilt. If you are living in violation or rebellion to God's laws—socially, naturally, or spiritually—then you are, in fact, guilty.

You may feel pressured, tense, apprehensive, or depressed. You may expect to hear bad news every time your phone rings. Perhaps you cannot sleep well at night. Unlikely people and situations may threaten you. Your sin may be fun, but the longer it lasts, the more miserable you feel.

Sin—that is, rebellion against God's law—is a two-sided coin: one side is fun temporarily, and the other side is misery.

God describes the guilty person in Isaiah 57:20-21. He says, "The wicked are like the troubled sea, when it cannot rest, whose waters cast up mire and dirt. There is no peace, saith my God, to the wicked."

Guilt will muddy the waters in your life. It shortens your temper, interferes with your digestion, and increases your blood pressure. Guilt literally brings out your worst traits.

As a result of sin, you may become an habitual liar, an uncontrollable drinker, a fornicator, a cheat, or a dishonest businessperson. You might simply become a loudmouth who is avoided by everybody. But one way or the other, real violation of God's principles will produce real guilt feelings and make you feel terrible.

Emotionally speaking, real guilt will wreck your mental health quicker than anything else you can do to yourself. Guilt feelings are more than the human mind and emotion can handle. Inside, we feel terrible any time we violate God's laws or the rights of other people. But even if we were the only person on earth, we would need to deal with guilt feelings in order to be happy.

Real guilt comes from violation of God's laws—morally, socially, and spiritually. And every person alive is guilty of all three violations. Not one of us can point an accusing finger at the other. My sins may differ in expression from yours, but they all come out of the same pot of spiritual rebellion.

Too often we human beings get hung up on clean and dirty sins—good and bad violations. While it is true that society categorizes sin because some are more socially devastating than others, in God's sight guilt has *one cause* and *one cure*.

The *cause* of guilt is rebellion against the bond God holds with you. The *cure* for guilt is in returning to God for unity. It is not the observance or violation of religious rules that condemn or justify us. Guilt comes from violating a relationship.

- Immorality violates intimate relationship with another person.
- Stealing violates our relationship with society.

- Murder violates another person's right to a relationship with life.
- Envy, strife, and hatred violate our rights and the rights of others to a relationship with happiness.
- Above all, guilt robs us of the spiritual oneness we desire with God, the Father of our eternal spirit.

This is what Jesus was talking about when He said He came to search for and save those who were lost. (See Luke 19:10).

Lost to what? A relationship with their Father in heaven.

Never mind what form of expression your guilt has taken to manifest itself. Never mind how long you may have been involved. You can be free from real guilt by a simple but definite decision to turn from the violations.

"Come now, and let us reason together, saith the Lord: though your sins be as scarlet, they shall be as white as snow; though they be red like crimson, they shall be as wool" (Isaiah 1:18). If you have been living without God, then you are guilty of sin. If you know God but you have been living in disobedience to His principles as stated in His Word, then you are guilty of sin.

If you are guilty and tired of it, then you can be free this very moment.

Are you guilty? Then do these three things:

1. Admit to yourself that you are in error, and resolve to abandon your wrong ways immediately.

33

2. Confess your sin to God.
3. Forget your sin, and reject all feelings of condemnation that may try to occupy your thoughts in the days to come.

FALSE GUILT

Some people feel guilty because they are guilty. Anytime we violate our relationship with God by sinning, we "feel" guilty—and we are guilty. And the only way we can get rid of real guilt feelings is to confess our sins and abandon them.

You will never feel right by doing wrong!

However, millions of Christian people, repentant and living in God's ways, actually "feel" more guilty than a seasoned criminal.

We counseled with a young Christian who came to us with such guilt feelings. When she first became born-again, she felt as though the whole world had suddenly turned rosy. She was happy, lighthearted, and eager to learn the Word and ways of God. She became active in church and was a great witness in the world. But one day she began to look back at the sinful life she had led before her commitment. Ironically, the realization of what she had actually been caused her to assume all the guilt feelings she should have experienced in her godless life-style.

As a result, this guilt-free young girl became so guilt conscious that it took two years of counseling, prayer, ministry, and teaching before her mind could be thoroughly renewed in this particular area of her thinking. Week after week we watched the light of truth battle with the darkness of error in her emotional and mental make-up.

She became nervous and afraid of being trapped in a crowd. Her heart began to palpitate. Night sweats and insomnia tormented her in the early morning hours. Indigestion set in. And, of course, her lively witness dried up like a shock of corn in autumn.

To realize what one has been or done should be a healthy experience for human beings. It is the mind's way of avoiding the same error. In looking back over my own mistakes, I could not believe I rationalized my sins to the point of actually being comfortable in them. But I did, and just like the young girl who came to us in despair, I felt condemned. With daily self-condemnation, I began to see myself as unworthy of the title "Christian."

It seemed that all other Christians were happy, holy, carefree, and bound for heaven. I was the only one guilty. And the irony of my plight was that I couldn't rid myself of guilt. I was like Shakespeare's character who tried to wash the murdered blood from her hands. Every day I looked back at my sins, reliving each miserable detail. Then I cried to God, saying, "Why don't You forgive me?"

God must have been crying back to me, "I have! Why don't you forgive yourself and stop reliving things I have already forgotten?"

What I did not realize at the time of my distress was that all the sins and mistakes of my past had been entirely forgiven. These guilt feelings were false. I was not, in fact, guilty. I only felt that way. Feelings—especially unstable feelings—lie more often than they tell the truth.

Real guilt comes from unconfessed sins and mistakes. *False guilt* is feeling condemned over what you have confessed to God and abandoned in practice.

God's Word says in 1 John 1:8-9, "If we say that we have no sin, we deceive ourselves, and the truth is not in us. If we confess our sins, he is faithful and just to forgive us our sins, and to cleanse us from all unrighteousness."

- Do you continually ask the Lord to forgive you for the same sin or sins?
- Are you frequently depressed over events of your past?
- Have you said, "What's the use trying?" and sunk deeper into depression?
- Do you readily condemn yourself?
- Do you try to punish yourself through excessively strict rules and self-denial?
- Does pointing out other people's faults make you feel better?
- Are you angry inside?
- Do you try to hide your guilt feelings by giving away more than you should? (I know people who give away money while unpaid bills lie overdue on their desk.)

If you answered "yes" to most of these questions, then you need to understand the nature of "false" guilt and how to stop feeding it.

To begin with, *feeling* guilty does not *make* you guilty. A person with a wounded mind or emotion will almost always "feel" guilty. Many times when we invite people to meet Jesus as their Savior and Lord, emotionally wounded men and women will later say they do not "feel" they have a relationship with God.

In one of his books, Dr. Ken Sumrall says he grew up under such fiery preaching that he got baptized three times! It sounds funny, but it is miserable to feel guilty every time someone points a finger.

False guilt will never rob you of God, but it can wreck your sense of peace with Him. The apostle Paul assured you and me that absolutely nothing can separate us from God's love. "Neither death, nor life ... nor principalities, nor powers, nor things present, nor things to come, nor height, nor depth...shall be able to separate us from the love of God, which is in Christ Jesus our Lord" (Romans 8:38-39).

Our relationship with our heavenly Father is absolutely secure in the Lord Jesus. Thank God our forgiveness does not depend on our fickle thoughts. Feelings, like the tide, come and go. I have yet to meet a stable person who charts his life by "feelings." People with sick emotions always have difficulty "sensing" the reality of truth.

"Feelings-bound" people have one primary thought, and that is *self*. If you spend the bulk of your time concentrating on yourself, your past, your sins, your fears, your loneliness, your sickness, your depression, your anxieties, your phobias, your hurts—your problems will seem more real to you than God because you know them so much better! *You will always know your mistakes better than you know forgiveness if you spend all your time with guilt.*

Do you see now, dear reader, that you cannot break the influence of your past if you insist on keeping in touch with it in your thoughts. This is like trying to break off a relationship with someone while you continue seeing them. It will not work.

If you want to be free of real guilt, confess your sin to God. Correct it with the person you have wronged (if it is wise to do so), then go about your business of living a new way—God's way. If you want to be free of guilt feelings—false guilt associated with your past—then you have got to stop thinking about them.

Basically, how you feel is the result of how you think, and only as you can control your thought life. Feelings make a poor compass. Only facts are dependable.

The fact is that you have made mistakes. The fact is also that God forgives sin. Now I want you to say out loud with me:

- "If I, (use your name), confess my sins, God is faithful and just to forgive my sins and to cleanse me from all unrighteousness." (See 1 John 1:9.)
- "I have confessed my sins to God in the Name of Jesus, therefore, I am no longer guilty."
- "Thank You, Lord Jesus, that Your death makes my life innocent."
- "I am not perfect. That is why Jesus died for me."
  - "My feelings sometimes lie. Therefore, from today, I will no longer depend on my feelings. From today, I will control my thoughts."

- "I am clean, forgiven, and whole. Thank You, Lord Jesus, that I am innocent."

Every time guilt feelings begin to accuse you, it will be up to you to stop their lies. You can do so by telling your thoughts the truth.

What is the truth? You are innocent!

This is precisely how I stopped my wounded, unstable feelings from lying to me and controlling my life. My mind has been entirely renewed on this point. I know I am innocent because I have convinced my mind by repeating the truth every time it needed a reminder.

4

Vain Imagination— Thought Replacement

One morning the phone rang for Paul. The well-known speaker we had invited and advertised—and were expecting in two days—had suddenly changed her mind. Her secretary expressed regrets at any inconvenience and hung up, leaving us holding the bag.

Anger, panic, frustration, accusation, and any number of unholy thoughts came pouring into my mind in those first few seconds. "Doesn't she realize that she has left us with no time to do anything?" I charged. "Why didn't you ask her why she waited until the last minute? You should have told her so and so," I rambled.

"Mona, she is not coming, and that's it!" Paul said matter-of-factly. "Two days from now we are going to have several hundred people looking for a special person, and they are going to get you and me."

A few hours passed and, in spite of my natural exasperation, I felt strangely peaceful. Paul and I prayed before going to bed that evening and committed the whole matter to God, asking Him to show us what to do the next day.

At ten o'clock the next morning, our phone rang for Paul a second time. It was our canceled guest's secretary. Our speaker would be coming after all. "God impressed us not to cancel your meeting," the cordial secretary assured us.

"She is coming?" I shouted.

"Yes," the Lord spoke at that moment. "But if your emotion had gotten hold of that phone yesterday, she would not be."

Then God brought a beautiful revelation of truth on this matter of people ruining their own plans. For the next few hours, the Lord showed me how emotional reactions often seal failure in our lives before He has had a chance to cause the situation to succeed.

You see, if Paul had reacted in anger toward that secretary and charged our invited guest with uncomplimentary adjectives, it would have been all over. And it would have been our fault that she did not show up. Given time, everything worked out beautifully.

Many people are going through life right now blaming other people for something they themselves caused by their own runaway thinking. An old, old story concerns just such a person. His name was Esau. You can read the story in Genesis 25:27-34.

Esau was a young, healthy outdoorsman. He was an expert marksman who went out one day to kill a deer so his elderly father could have some venison. Since he was the oldest son, Esau was going to receive his father's blessing following the meal. This meant he would inherit both the spiritual and financial leadership of the family tribe.

Esau was gone several hours past his meal time. When he finally came back home, his blood sugar level had undoubtedly dropped quite low. He said to his younger brother, Jacob, "I feel like I am going to faint."

It just so happened that Jacob was outside their tent making lentil soup. "Give me some of your soup," Esau requested.

"Give me your birthright," Jacob responded, "and I will give you some of my soup."

Now get ready to view a classic case of someone who is about to ruin his future inheritance because of runaway thinking. "What good is my inheritance since I am at the point to die?" Esau reasoned. So he sat down and ate Jacob's bargain.

Remember, the story says that Esau was an outdoorsman. He was young, strong, and healthy. In reality, he was nowhere near death. He only had a drop in blood sugar. The Bible says that as soon as he ate, he "rose up and went his way."

One minute Esau was in panic, about to die; and, after one bowl of soup, he was completely restored. Jacob did not take Esau's birthright from him—rather, Esau's runaway thoughts stole it.

Runaway thinking is a robber. Many good plans go down the drain simply because we do not exercise self-control. And self-control begins in the mind that *acts* instead of *reacts* to its circumstances. Actions, not reactions, keep a situation under control.

A young pastor we know fell into adultery when one of his attractive parishioners came to him for counseling wearing very skimpy clothing. Instead of acting in the best interest of that emotionally unstable girl and sending her home for more appropriate attire, he lost control of his thoughts and destroyed a church. Obviously, there was more to the situation than clothing. But action on that point would have sent a definite signal to the girl's flesh as well as to the pastor's own unruly passions.

Our natural tendency to react and lose the benefit of seeing a situation through to maturity is one reason God placed several spiritual prescriptions in His Word addressing the matter of sound thinking.

For example, the apostle Peter wrote, "Wherefore gird up the loins of your mind, be sober..." (1 Peter 1:13). That is, keep your thoughts under control.

The word "gird" comes from the same word as girdle. In ancient times when men wore robes, they never went anywhere without a girdle. A girdle was a linen belt (or leather if you were poor) that was tied at the waist to keep a flowing robe from interfering with a person's mobility.

Just imagine how cumbersome a robe flapping around your knees or ankles would be—how easily you might trip and fall. What a hindrance to your everyday activities.

Unruly, undisciplined, and uncontained thoughts are like these beltless robes. They cause you to walk clumsily through life breaking the fine things God has set on the shelf for you to purchase.

Yes, you have to choose self-control. You have to purchase sound thinking, and the currency you use is called will power. You have to submit to mental and emotional renewal just the way our present home had to cooperate with the renovation we did. Not one wall refused to fall when we took the hammer to it. Not one heater refused to dry up, once we closed off the valves. With minimum objection, our house cooperated with the daily changes.

"Gird up the loins of your mind" tells us that will power is involved in how we think. Runaway thoughts expose a will too lazy to engage in renovation. However harsh it may sound, it is true!

Many people with emotional trouble have problems because of a lazy will. They simply do not want to put forth the effort it takes to carve a new way of thinking and acting. It takes just as much effort to "think" right as it does to "act" right. Many people find it easier to flow with whatever feeling is present: "Why fight it?"

Well, I fought it because I hated being miserable, and I disliked being afraid to leave home without my tranquilizers. I fought runaway thoughts because they continually robbed my life of good plans and good people. I continue to fight as often as necessary because I enjoy being happy. I never leave home now without my girdle. That is, I guard my thoughts continually.

CONTROLLING YOUR IMAGINATION

In the last chapter we introduced the possibility of renewing the mind through "thought control." Every person who has excessive emotional or mental distress is a victim of runaway thoughts and imagination. Before we go on to another specific area of problem emotion, let's stop for a minute and pursue this possibility of taking control of thoughts and feelings through *thought replacement*.

One day I overheard Paul in conversation with someone. He was attempting to bring reason into a young woman's emotions. She kept saying, "I feel like I am going crazy."

"But feelings lie," Paul kept repeating. "Don't listen to that kind of thinking. Replace those thoughts with what Jesus said about you. You can do all things through Christ, who strengthens you." (See Philippians 4:13.)

"But I don't feel like doing anything."

"Do it anyway," Paul encouraged her. "Call up a friend, go out and have lunch together—get out. Tell somebody about Jesus. Help somebody. Get involved with life outside your own small world."

What Paul was saying is absolutely true. Replacing miserable thoughts with encouraging thoughts is one of the vital secrets to improving your mental attitude. You can discipline your mind. It is possible to throw away all those thoughts that make you miserable, that you can take control of your imagination. These are necessities to restoring sound thinking.

Stop listening to your unsound ways of occupying your mind. No person in heaven or on earth is going to override your will or tamper with your hearing aid. Mental discipline is up to you. It is that simple—simple, but not easy when your emotions are walking around inside you like a wounded lion.

Misery takes frequent strolls between the mind, body, and spirit of the person who is struggling to hold together. Your head feels light, one-sided, and dizzy—like liquid metal shifting from side to side. Your stomach pumps like a little golf ball but feels bloated to the size of a melon. You imagine your heart will stop one foot beyond your doorstep, and you envision every eye beaming toward you saying, "Hey, everybody, look! There goes somebody nervous."

It is not easy to go outside your home when you think you are the leading star of every shopping center, grocery store, city bus, or public gathering. I once heard a minister of a five thousand member church tell how he choked, sweated, and trembled during the months he was experiencing a nervous breakdown. People he had always known and loved suddenly became a major threat to him. But he did just what I am telling you to do. He fought the lying feelings. He did not give in to them.

Instead of going home and locking himself inside his house, he continued to minister each Sunday morning in the very face of his tormenting fears and trembling. He risked falling apart in front of everybody. Finally he came out of it. It was painful. It did not happen overnight, but day by day. One step at a time that minister renewed his unrealistic imagination by replacing its erroneous thinking with a healthy view of reality.

The human imagination has tremendous ability. From the time we are born, we set out to develop it. Little girls put on mamma's high-heeled shoes and imagine they are grown up. Little boys get daddy's razor and shave themselves into manhood.

47

All our lives we use our imagination to escape the day-to-day drudgery in which we sometimes find ourselves. When pressures get too heavy for me, I go by the travel bureau and look at all the sunshiny places I could go to get away from everything. Of course, I rarely take such a vacation, but I like to imagine the interesting things I would learn if I did. Other people imagine themselves as famous sports figures. Some people learn about gourmet cooking in France. Others look at new positions available in the want ads.

I call this innocent imagination. Another way we use our imagination is in creating something new—new equipment, new music, new books, new medical advances, new ways of improving society, etc. Out of our imagination have come comfortable cars, planes, trains, ships, television sets, dishwashers, and electric lights. Yes, I remember when we burned oil lamps and did most things with common elbow grease. But because of man's constructive imagination, we have many wonderful conveniences in almost every country of the world.

However, as wonderful as the imagination may be, it has two essential flaws in it:

1. The human imagination can produce bad as well as good.
2. Our imagination, like a computer, knows only what we feed it.

Therefore, an imagination not under the control of God will definitely arrive at a number of false conclusions. For example, suppose someone hurts you. You think it over, and you are innocent. Hate is justified, so you refuse to speak to him or her for the rest of your life. This way, you *imagine* you can get even with him.

A family with whom we were well-acquainted bears out this point. The father and young son had an argument over a boat and stopped speaking. The months grew into five silent years between them. I am quite sure it was a time of considerable imagination against each other. After five years, the silence was sealed forever when the father died unexpectedly.

An imagination without God draws too many painful conclusions. If we did not imagine that we were perfect, we could tolerate each other's weaknesses more readily. If we did not imagine that we are called to administer vengeance, we could release arguments and differing opinions to God and let Him teach others the lessons they need to hear.

If some people did not imagine that the world owes them a living, they would get a job and stick with it. They would stop writing bad checks and stealing.

CASTING DOWN IMAGINATIONS

Do you know people who inspire you to say, "Oh, no, here comes trouble," as soon as you see them approaching? People who carry trouble with them do not have God in control of their imagination. They forever fabricate lies and brew division.

Imaginations that assume there is no God or that His Word is a joke rewrite the moral codes of society. They produce dirty books, immoral television programs and movies, and the freaky noise some people call music.

But what about those of us who may not be thieves; or hate filled, or pornographers, or have our hair dyed green? We may be simply filling our minds with painful suspicion and imagination.

We imagine every laugh is at us. We imagine every whisper is about us. We imagine every word is directed toward us.

Do you ever "feel" like you don't belong with people? Do you imagine that nobody likes you, people are out to get you, or people only want to use you?

Are you afraid people want to make a fool of you?

These are all vain imaginings. They are not born of God; but arise out of your own natural conclusions and are based on the suggestions of a sick imagination. And while Satan is the "father of lies," he can feed unreality only to a mind that is *willing* to listen.

God's spiritual prescription for a miserable imagination is this: Cast down imaginations that exalt themselves against the knowledge (mind) of God, and bring into captivity every thought to the obedience of Christ. (See 2 Corinthians 10:5.)

When God's Word says that you and I are to "cast down imaginations," that phrase "cast down" literally means in the original text to "violently demolish." Now you see that the idea of throwing away thoughts is not mine but God's. Rise up like an angry tiger and say to your miserable thinking, "I am taking control of you. You have made me miserable for the last time." You will then see those old misery-producing feelings begin to back away and run.

God did not tell you to do something impossible. If He said you and I can throw out specific thoughts that lie and steal our happiness, then we *are* able to do it. In a day when you can get rid of almost anything at the snap of a finger, don't tell me you cannot demolish a cowardly little thing like a thought.

The problem with most of us is that we have been intimidated by our unsound imaginations. Thousands of healthy people are sitting around waiting for a heart attack. Others are sitting on unfulfilled dreams because the plane might crash. Some are too stingy to part with a nickel because of impending financial collapse. Our minds crust over with one imagined disaster after another. Consequently, we go through our lives with thoughts directly opposed to the powerful, happy, and liberated thinking of faith-filled people.

It is possible to cast down and utterly demolish all fear-filled, hate-filled, and doubt-filled, untrue thoughts that come into your imagination. You can get rid of thoughts that do not agree with God's estimate of you. You can eradicate thoughts that do not agree with God's Word to you, along with thoughts that doubt God's concern for you. You can learn to think about yourself the same way God thinks about you and all of life's circumstances.

Why don't we stop right here and introduce some areas of problem imagination common to most of us and see how we may redirect our minds into new patterns of thinking.

Start first with marriage. A vain imagination has ruined many potentially good marriages. I remember one such example that surfaced one evening in Puerto Rico when several couples had gathered at the home of an American executive for dinner. A good time was well under way, as dinner parties go, when the telephone rang. Several minutes later the wife of the host executive came down the stairs, all color drained from her face, crying, "George has another woman." The truth was that we all had known it long before the brokenhearted wife found out. Because George imagined that he was God's gift to women, he spent every evening at one of the ritzy bars making a fool of himself with adventure-seeking tourists who wanted a free drink or a night on the town.

On the other hand, a girl I went to school with imagined she could have more fun out of life if she left her husband and two small children to become a part of the liberated drug scene. A few years later, her body was found beaten to death after one of those "fun" evenings.

You never fool anybody but yourself when you imagine to cheat without consequence on the sacred vows you exchange in marriage. The ways of cheating a partner are as endless as our ability to think. Husbands and wives who refuse each other's reasonable affection and imagine that they are getting by with it only fool themselves. Marriage is a mystical union created by God. Any violation of that union causes both parties to suffer whether or not the matter is ever brought into open discussion.

A friend of mine landed what she thought was a big catch, and we all agreed she had hooked the bachelor of the century. After several months of marriage, my friend began to experience emotional disorders. She grew more and more confused and unsure of herself. A couple of years went by; and, to everybody's amazement, she packed her things and moved out. What had happened to the ideal couple in the ideal town who lived in the ideal house? Her husband had imagined when he married her that she would never consent to consummate the marriage with a physical relationship. He imagined that she would remain perfectly content to lie beside him at night while he dreamed of men or some other perverse sexual outlet.

A couple came to us one evening with the ridiculous excuse that the wife could not participate in intimate relationship for the past nine years because she was afraid. After twenty years of marriage, she became afraid of sex.

"What are you afraid of?"

"I don't know," she said, as she mumbled some lame excuse for her unthinkable conduct. "My husband is a good man. I just don't know."

No doubt, a long season of counseling would uncover some quirks in that woman's imagination. But I know from personal experience that a mind can be made to obey orders just as surely as a child is disciplined. I am convinced that a woman with a good husband can bring her thoughts under control to the point of fulfilling her responsibilities to her marriage, if she will.

You have to *will* good things into your mind. You have to *will* good things into your life. I am amazed at how many of us let our minds lead us around like spoiled brats. If you have a ridiculous imagination about your good husband or good wife, then you need to replace your vain mind with sound thoughts. You have the authority of your own personal will to administer the discipline.

Imagining that you can secretly or openly violate the marriage commitment and still find happiness is like tearing off one wing of a plane and telling yourself it will still fly.

Do not imagine that you can be hateful to your partner and get love. Stop hoping for a compliment if you are a slob. If your favorite perfume is body odor, don't be shocked when a television rerun is preferred. We must stop our foolish and perverse imagination and admit to what we are, if we ever hope to get help in our situation.

A method of humanity I have observed is this: We each have our little area of specialty in life. One knows law, one farming, one science, one manufacturing, one retailing, and so forth. Yet, because we are knowledgeable of our little specialty, we think we can deceive and cut corners with the less knowledgeable. We think they will never know the difference.

How foolish! I do not have to know a particular line of work to sense when someone is telling me a lie. Deception comes out of the spirit and is spiritually interpreted.

When buildings collapse, you don't need an architect to tell you somebody cut corners in the construction. When some person sells you a valuable item that loses its worth at the next appraiser, you don't need an expert to tell you the first man lied.

What vain imagination we allow ourselves as we deal with one another. When will we become honest? I am speaking to Christians now. God tells us to "speak every man truth" with ourselves and with each other. (See Ephesians 4:25.)

You can control what you do.

You can control what you say.

You can control what you think.

If your life is miserable or your imagination is the cause of marital misery, it is up to you to help yourself develop a new way of being. I am not talking about becoming a Christian. I am talking about Christians becoming sound in their thinking.

CHOOSING HEALTHY THOUGHTS

One afternoon Paul and I walked into Kennedy International Airport to board a plane for Greece. I was overworked and emotionally spent. The moment we stepped into the terminal I heard a voice so loud it produced immediate nausea in the pit of my stomach.

"You are weak!" the voice said. "Why don't you stop trying to save the world and just go home like other women."

"I have to find a restroom," I said to my husband. Following the signs while he checked the luggage, I went into a stall, got on my knees (yes, in a dirty bathroom), and said, "Lord, I need help!"

"You can do all things through Christ, who gives you strength!" I heard in my spirit right near the place I was nauseated. (See Philippians 4:13.)

I got to my feet, still weak, afraid, and uncertain, but I began to repeat what I had heard. "I can do all things through Christ who strengthens me." "I can do all things through Christ." "I can do all things."

At that moment I heard two opposing thoughts. I could choose whichever I willed. But if I had not chosen to replace the first thought with the second good Word, I would have missed three great weeks in Greece,

Israel, and England, plus all the wonderful experiences that transpired during our visit.

Who controls your life, you or your thoughts?

Are there things you would like to do or become, but, after you think it over, you usually tell yourself "no"? Are there habits, sins, or lifestyles you would like to quit, but you keep saying "yes" to them? Do you know how to tell irritating people where to get off, but never do the same with your own harassing imagination?

If so, you can renew your mind and reform its way of using time. You can do with a thought the same thing you can do with an unwanted house guest—throw it out! An attractive, young girl came to us who was hung up on oral copulation. On one hand, she hated herself and was threatening suicide; on the other, she received great pleasure from her obsession. As long as she came regularly to learn a new way of thinking, she made progress. When she ceased to attend our teaching sessions, she gradually slipped back into her old lifestyle and was again consumed with a degrading, futureless way of letting people use her.

Obsessions, habits, phobias, fears, and all aggressive, destabilizing thoughts cannot be corrected overnight, short of a miracle. One counseling session or one good Bible-based teaching in these cases is tantamount to taking an aspirin for cancer. You have to fight for freedom in your mind, and you have to do it as often and as long as necessary. You can win! But one battle is not sufficient.

Let us take a step now in the direction you must go if you will find long-lasting mental and emotional renewal through thought replacement. I want you to say and do the following peace producers as often as necessary:

- I *can* control my thoughts!
- I *will* control my thoughts!
- I will think God's thoughts today! (You will find God's thoughts in the Bible.)
- I will stop every unhealthy thought that comes to my mind. I will not entertain miserable thinking!
- Thank You, Jesus, for a healthy imagination. Thank You for giving me an imagination that blesses me as well as other people!
- I now dedicate my imagination to God for good!

The best place I have found to turn my imagination loose for good is to get into the study of God's Word. If you want to stretch your thoughts to exciting possibilities, let Jesus fill you full of His way of thinking and acting.

You may see your physical possibilities as being very limited, and they may be small. But spiritually speaking, you can become a giant. God has no limit to what He can and will do through even the weakest person who fully surrenders his mind to Him.

5

Rejection

For five years, Paul and I traveled continually in the United States and abroad sharing our music and personal Christian experiences.

In all those years of moving on the spur of the moment—catching late-night trains, sleeping in air terminals, and going from house to house—one lesson we learned quickly was the cost of excess baggage. Every extra bag was a hassle.

The emotional parallel of this travel experience is similar to the hassle of every unnecessary thought and mental hang-up we drag through life. In fact, emotional weights will wear you out more quickly than extra luggage. It is wearisome to struggle through each day pulling three or four anxiety thoughts alongside you.

The joy of being alive will soon evaporate for those travelers who don't learn to repack their way of thinking and discard all unnecessary mental burdens. I am not talking about a one-time mental cleanup. I am referring to a new way of living, with frequent emotional releases that develop a new way of seeing yourself and your life in relationship to other people.

God, our designer, the One who created our intricate emotional balance, tells us to lay aside every weight and sin that easily upsets us. (See Hebrews 12:1.) This assures us that it is possible. You can eliminate all the mental garbage you have collected over the years and free your mind to carry only what is necessary for your happiness today.

In this chapter, I want to take a look at an attitude or "weight" that drains the life out of many people without their realizing it. This multifaceted emotion is called "rejection."

One way or another, most of us spend our lives trying to measure up to some other person's expectations of us in order to avoid the pains of rejection. A family name, twentieth-century advertising, fashions, or fads—we all feel pressured to become what someone else says we should become, look the way someone else says we should look, or like what someone else says is preferable.

For example, some common family expectations might go like this: "Your brother had already gone into his profession at your age; your sister already has her own business. Of course, we understand you have never gotten your case together."

"You are the only family member who can't carry a tune—you never did have an ear for music."

"You have always been disorganized."

"The others made the honor roll."

"You were never coordinated. Remember how athletic Bobby was?"

"Your cousins always look like models—of course, you can't help having big ankles."

"But son, your father will be so disappointed if you become a preacher."

Then advertisers come along with hallucinations about dream men, dream women, and dream worlds. With a very clever approach, they make the whole world feel inferior unless they rush out to buy a certain product.

- No sports car—no girl.
- No breath mint—no kiss.
- No mouth wash—no romance.
- No dandruff shampoo—nobody will sit
  beside you on the bus.
- Wrong coffee—no marriage.

If you are a woman, the pressure is really on to measure up!

- One thousand calories a day.
- Size 10 only.
- Invite that handsome man over for a drink.
  He'll stay, and you'll live happily ever
  after.
- Buy the right detergent and gain your
  mother-in-law's favor.
- Of course, if you don't use the right perfume,
  you are never going to get a mother-in-law
  anyway.

With family pressures saying "measure-up" and daily advertising pressures saying "hurry-up!" it is no wonder we feel drained, insecure, and rejected. What our family has not pointed out through comparisons, our television set has challenged through larger-than-life fantasy living.

But God saw the twentieth century coming, and He gave us the remedy for the pressures of the human measuring stick. He said simply, "Set aside the weight. Chuck the pressures."

For years I sweated from one season to the next wondering if I would be in style enough to attend my fancy Sunday school class. Could I afford to adapt my wardrobe the way fashion said I needed to? My friends and I lived with a tape measure in one hand and the weekend fashion column in the other. I always dreaded the change of season because my clothes inevitably fell short of perfect coordination. Color combinations, glove length—somehow I never quite measured up.

What a wonderful release occurred the day I was liberated from fashion nonsense. I try to look nice now, but it is because I want to, not because a thought connected to a pencil says I should do this or that if I want to be in style.

Furthermore, I adapt as I choose. Women may blow a fuse again someday and run around in dresses that look like a dog ripped off the bottom, but I will never again let designers shrink my good taste to mini-size. How ridiculous! Women in Boston were running around in bottomless dresses and coats in ten degree weather trying to avoid fashion rejection. Conformity to the extreme fashions of today represent the same fears.

Regardless of how intelligent, rich, famous, or hand-some we are, all of us have experienced the pains of re-jection at some time in our lives. And we will do almost anything to avoid a repeat performance. It hurts to be rejected. It hurts to have your ideas tossed aside at work. It hurts to have your in-laws reject you. It hurts to have your husband or wife think you are stupid, and it hurts to have your children be ashamed of you after you have given a big portion of your life for them.

One day I called a neighbor of mine at her office. The secretary answered the phone, and I could hear her say-ing to my neighbor, "It's Mona Johnian calling."

Then I heard my neighbor's voice reply in a disgust-ed tone, "I don't want to speak to her!"

I was hurt! I wanted to cry or crack her head open, and both options seemed fair game. "Who does that lit-tle self-centered, ambitious, ten-cent millionaire think she is?" I said indignantly.

Before my emotions were renewed, I often went around grinding such axes as this incident with my neighbor. Having grown up in a financially comfortable family, I was popular in school and accepted in my par-ticular circle. I found it extremely painful to have the boss yell, the policeman fume, the neighbor ignore me, the country club say "no," or a promotion be delayed— or to find an unappreciative response to my goodwill. It made life appear full of rejections. And in truth, it is.

The reasons for rejection are as varied and versatile as our reason for success. Some rejection is real, and some is imagined. Many people imagine that others are against them when, in fact, they are not. Have you ever spent time with people who think everybody is out to reject them? They are so paranoid you have to choose each word with utmost caution to avoid offending them.

People suffering from suspected rejection are suspicious, analytical, critical, and gossipy over the actions of others. They are not only in pain, but they are pains to live with.

Yet, much of the rejection we suffer is real.

A young man came to talk with us one evening. He was suffering from years of rejection by his father. Although his father loved him, their personalities were so different from each other that they were worlds apart in communication. The father had a driving, peopleless, materialistic mentality. He was brilliant in ability and ruthless in relationships. The son, on the other hand, had a sensitive, people-conscious, helping nature and was of average mental ability.

Taking the normal pattern of children and human nature, the young boy tried to gain his father's approval by rejecting his own personality. When we talked to him, the young man was a hard-nosed, insensitive, lawless young man on the outside; and he hated the fact that he was jelly through and through in his heart.

God showed me his problem a short time after he began to pour out his innermost personality. "You have buried the real you," I said to the young man. "And if you want to get your case together, you have to start digging in search of your real nature. You have tried to assume your father's personality, and it's not working."

Frustrated, confused, miserable, and making everybody else the same way, that young man did begin the painful process of digging out his own heart and mind from beneath the mounds of rejection. After four years, he was able to resurrect his real personality and enter the profession of his choice. He gained peace with himself, his father, and the people around him.

Real or imagined, we will be confronted with what appears to us as rejection as long as we live. I was watching Barbara Walters being interviewed on television one evening. To my surprise, she said, "Yes, I get rejected. Nobody knows how many people say 'no' to my invitations for an interview. But I never take stock in the rejections. I simply look for the one who will say, 'yes.'"

In other words, she copes well with her professional rejections, and her career continues to survive. If you learn to cope with your rejections, you also will survive and become successful.

Let us go back for a moment to the incident where I called my neighbor and she refused to speak to me. Since this event occurred after I had begun my venture into good emotional health, I determined not to let it rob me of my peace of mind. At first I was tempted to resent my neighbor and "pay her back." But then I said, "No, Lord, I turn this situation over to you, and I ask you to teach me your lesson from it."

Do you want to know what God showed me? It was a bit painful, but He liberated me from a life-long false assumption. Over the next few days following that incident, I came to realize several things about this dramatic emotion we call rejection.

1. I became honest with myself. First, I was surprised to realize that I was just as "self-centered" as my neighbor. When she refused to talk to me, it was because I represented no gain to her. She was a building contractor; at that time I was in the arts. But the truth was, I only wanted to talk to her about something that would benefit my career. I wanted something out of her. In all honesty, I hardly even liked the woman. Therefore, my first step toward healing in that situation was to become honest with myself.

I was self-centered, proud, and ambitious. In addition to my super-sensitive preoccupation with success, I nursed a debilitating load of self-pity. I was like a toy cap pistol subject to fire at any moment.

2. I thought mostly of myself. The second thing I admitted was that I spent most of my time thinking about myself, which is contrary to God's rules for good mental health. Jesus' summation of happiness and fulfillment is to prefer one another and esteem others better than yourself. (See Philippians 2:3.) This is excellent mental and emotional therapy for the rejected.

Did you ever hurt your toe, and it seemed that every person walking by stepped on it? That is because you had your toe uppermost in your mind. You probably did not get stepped on any more than usual—it just seemed that way when all your thoughts were centered on your toe.

If you live with yourself as the star and measure every situation by what it means to you, then you are going to experience the pains of rejection continually.

On the other hand, you can operate by the principles Jesus set down and find continual release from the wounds inflicted by others:

- Seek to *accept* rather than to be *accepted*, and leave other's responses to God.
- Seek to *love* more than to *be loved*. Seek to give rather than to get.
- Seek to *be used* rather than to *use*. Seek to become a servant more than a master.

In other words, the miracle therapy for rejected people is to become *givers*—givers of themselves, their time, and their goods.

I believe life has perfect balance within it right now. Jesus said that the Kingdom of God is within us. For every rejected person is a person in need waiting to be loved and accepted. What we need is to get into the marketplace of life and find those places and people who need what we have to offer.

GIVING WITHOUT IMPOVERISHMENT

You may be saying to yourself, "I do try to reach out and give, but few people seem to appreciate my sacrifice."

To that I say, "You are absolutely right." Not everybody appreciates goodwill. But God takes care of that emotional reaction with a brilliant principle stated in Colossians 3:23: "Whatsoever ye do, do it heartily as to the Lord, and not unto men." That way your labor will not be in vain.

How completely thorough are God's ways. His backup systems are superb. When someone rejects your good intentions and shows no appreciation for something that may have cost you great effort, you can respond positively.

When I am rejected, I simply go to the Lord. I cry if I need to. I forgive the person by saying so out loud. Then I turn the whole situation over to God for proper storage. I remind myself that the work was for God and not man, and God appreciates my sacrifice. With the mental atmosphere clear above my heart, I then ask God to refocus my present *purpose* and *responsibilities,* and I get busy.

Up to this point, I have used the term "suffer from rejection" several times. I do this because I want to make a point. All people *experience* rejection throughout their life. It is the people who do not know how to *cope* who suffer the full extent of the experience. *Rejection is inevitable, but suffering from rejection is a matter of choice.*

3. I was guilty of rejecting others. I have chosen to live happily in the midst of other people's good or bad intentions because I came to realize that *I was as guilty as anyone else of rejecting others.* Many people came to my mind who had reached out to me in some way but had gotten nowhere. I had hurt countless people and hardly even acknowledged their existence. Rejection is the nature of *self-centered humanity.*

But the good news is that we can each be liberated from having to fit someone else's pattern. We can become victor instead of victim of life's real or imagined rejections. A fair and just measuring stick exists by which we may judge our situations.

The only comparison important enough to me today is how I live my life in relationship to my heavenly Father. He is the only standard by which you and I will be judged in the final analysis.

If your life pleases God—by measuring up to His Word and will for you—then you are in style, period; and so is your house and all your possessions.

Years ago, when I first left home, I went out and bought draperies for my living room. With off-white walls I proudly hung my green floral prints, which also had an off-white background. I thought the room belonged in *House Beautiful* until someone came along and informed me that printed draperies break up the lines in a small room—I should have chosen solid curtains the color of my walls. From that day forward I hated those draperies and was self-conscious for anybody to see the broken line in my living room.

In that ritzy Sunday school class I once attended, I remember a pretty young woman who created secret envy in the heart of every female among us. Added to her natural beauty was a wealthy husband who dressed her like a princess. If she wore a yellow dress, she also wore yellow shoes. She had a yellow handbag and yellow gloves—if they had made yellow lip stick, I'm sure her smile would have been yellow, too. Oh, how uncoordinated we impoverished fashion buffs felt.

How foolish! How emotionally bound we all were. Of our fashion-bound camaraderie, three got divorces, three had emotional breakdowns, and one is still reading the fashion columns' newest fantasy. Even the girl in yellow divorced her Prince Charming. We each fell apart in our own way because we were using the wrong measuring stick. Not one of us understood that the favor we were really seeking was God's. We needed to know deep inside our hearts that we were accepted. We needed to know that we did make-the-grade where it counted.

God-confidence is the only way I have found to tie down all those intimidating fears inflicted by people who are just as afraid and rejected as I am. God-confidence is the one assurance that makes me know I belong wherever God puts me, regardless of people's opinions.

From the fashion industry to competitive business, career mistakes, and overspending in your family, trying to impress the world is a miserable fantasy. Living to be accepted by the world is an impossible ambition. We have all done it. We have all suffered from it. But it is a wonderful feeling to know you can recover quickly from it. And the secret is God-confidence—doing whatever you do because your innermost spirit desires it.

It is a great liberty to be free to give without having to have someone call out the brass band for you. Just to know that the Lord knows and you desire His favor is sufficient. That is emotional and mental renewal that can never be taken from you. No one can escape rejection, but anyone with right understanding can avoid its wounds.

6

Release From Things

Have you ever stopped to consider how much emotion is tied up in material things? A friend of ours was getting ready to leave for a visit with his family when he dented the fender of his car. That one relatively insignificant event caused him to cancel all his plans and leave everybody disappointed.

People have stopped speaking to each other over tire marks on a lawn, a borrowed item of clothing, or a piece of lost jewelry. Every day you read in the newspaper where some person risked his or her life to retrieve $30.00 from a would-be robber.

What is this mysterious fascination for things that causes people to steal, overwork, destroy their health, step on people, or neglect their families just to possess material objects? Some people are thieves, but most of us are only prisoners to the tangible things of this world.

That is what this chapter is all about—liberating your mind from the pressures of materialism and being set free from over-concern with the temporary provisions of this life.

We should acknowledge, first of all, that life has a certain amount of need. We must have somewhere to sleep, food to eat, and clothing to protect our bodies from the elements. And since God created everything beautiful on this earth, we have every reason to make our natural life as attractive as possible—within reason.

Therefore, I am not proposing neglecting or abusing our natural gifts in life. I believe the opposite. We are responsible to be grateful and to manage properly the things with which we are blessed. What I am talking about is our constant preoccupation in building little kingdoms for ourselves and striving to hold onto our grand image-makers. I am addressing the mentality that allows advertisers to make billions of dollars a year with such words as "New," "Exciting," "Better," "Satisfying," and "Exotic."

We are talking about how to renew our minds. Remember, the word "renew" means to *renovate*, and renovate means to improve. God assures you and me that it is possible to improve our way of thinking. He gives us the prescription in Ephesians 4:23,28: "Be renewed (renovated) in the spirit of your mind.... Let him that stole steal no more: but rather let him labour, working with his hands the thing which is good, that he may have to give to him that needeth."

You may be saying to yourself, "I don't steal." Fine. (In case you do steal, your solution is quite simple: get a job and start giving away all you don't need!) The point I am making here is that the same obsession for things that drives a person to steal drives you and me to be overly concerned with "what we will eat, what we will wear, and where we will live!" Jesus told us this was our number one priority.

Since we definitely have to have things in order to live, what we want to learn is how to keep them in balance—how to master instead of being mastered and possess instead of being possessed. As always, God provides the prescription for our exaggerations.

In Hosea 14:3, God says we are to come to Him and confess, "Neither will we say any more to the work of our hands, Ye are our gods...."

What? Things can become gods?

Yes, "things" are not just objects for sale in the markets of life. *Things* have a real potential to become gods. *Things* want to be served. Things desire to be the object of your affection—rather, the *spirit* behind things desires this allegiance. It is not unusual for people to worship things seven days a week. Take a look at the new, greedy retail policy that has finally succeeded in abolishing Sunday as a family day of worship and recreation. Malls and stores open every day of the week, fishing for every dollar they can pull in. But, of course, they could not operate without customers, could they? This is visual evidence of "things" worship.

The whole of society is mad with materialistic acquisitions. Unfortunately, this has always been the case. Even thousands of years ago, during Nehemiah's time, God warned His people not to go out and buy the flea marketer goods on the Sabbath. The obvious reason was that He did not want them to become worshipers of things or slaves to the temporary. (See Nehemiah 10:31.) "Things" have spiritual power behind them. They have the potential to become gods. Unless you are aware, things can be a real bondage in your life.

My husband Paul and I both used to value our possessions far above people. We dreaded company for fear they would dirty the carpets, fingerprint the walls, and rearrange the scatter pillows. One of the greatest releases of our lives was liberation from our house.

God sent us so much company, once we surrendered to the liberation process, that Paul threatened to put a cross on the roof. God moved us, flooded our apartment, and had rats chew our furniture in storage—anything and everything to liberate us from materialistic bondage.

Most Christians take Jesus' commission to "watch" as meaning to guard their precious belongings. "Jesus may be coming soon, but I'm keeping an eye on my new necklace."

Let me ask you something: When you leave home, do you worry about your things? If so, then you *carry* stress with you.

When you are home, are you overly concerned with how things look? If so, then you live with stress. (I'm not talking about being dirty. We need to keep reasonable order.) In your home, which do you value more, things or people? Is it difficult for you to accommodate guests in your home? If so, then every knock at the door sparks stress inside you.

Are you conscious of what others have that you do not? Does it bother you? Be honest. During a day's time, do your thoughts turn more to God or what you look like, what you have on, or what you are going to eat for supper? I want us to stop here and spend a moment liberating our minds from the stresses of our material possessions. Do you know that one day you are going to surrender all of them? Why not today? That way you can enjoy living!

First of all, God gives us the key to liberty from materialism in His Ephesian prescription. Let's take it. Work with your hands that you may have to give to the person who is in need.

The purpose of "goods" is not to store them up in your attic or bank vault, but to give them away. *Giving* is the key to releasing your life from obsessive hoarding and the accompanying stresses.

At age fifty, John D. Rockefeller, Sr., became so ill he was not expected to live. On his sick bed, he made a conscious decision to become a giver (he had already been a Christian for many years). He started giving away in numerous directions; and, as a result, he recovered and lived forty years longer.

Stress was killing him. Excessive concern for things put him in bed, but *giving* brought him out of it!

You, too, can be delivered from materialistic stress. I want you to take a step in that direction right now. Say out loud:

- Everything I have is just a temporary pos session to meet my temporary needs.
- Everything I have was given to me through God's favor. Therefore, every thing I have really belongs to God.
- I can trust God to take care of His things.

- I will stop worrying about the things I
  own. Even if I lose them, it will not be
  the end of the world.
- I can be happy with less than I possess be
  cause my happiness is not dependent
  on things.
- Today I dedicate every single thing I own
  to God.
- I will give away anything and everything
  as God directs me. And He will reward me with all I need.

Say this every day until you mean it. Then act on
what God tells you to do. Great liberty awaits you!

RELEASE YOUR HAPPINESS

A second consideration in renewing your mind concerning "things" is this: Most people spend their lives
postponing happiness in favor of their things.

To paraphrase some of Jesus' liberating words,
"Don't be anxious about tomorrow. God will take care
of your tomorrow, too. Live one day at a time." (See Matthew 6:34.)

Obviously, His instruction was not designed to turn
us into careless people who throw everything to the
wind, living as though there is no God, no tomorrow,
and no responsibilities in life. It was a statement to help
worriers and overplanners learn to live today.

Most people spend their lives planning happiness,
but they rarely ever live it. We plan a big celebration.
Then someone spills ketchup on our white suit. We get

the flu, or the basement floods, and we end up disappointed or cancel the celebration altogether.

We plan to enjoy our family during vacation, but the kids fight in the back seat of the car, the air-conditioning breaks down, and mosquitoes invade the campsite.

We plan to do some good inspirational reading during the summer, but instead we have a two-month sinus attack, the fence needs mending, or we build a rock garden.

We promise to take the children to see Mickey Mouse, attend their school programs, and listen to their little ideas, but we keep saying, "Wait just a minute," until they have gone to college.

We plan to call that special person, send them a card, or surprise them with a little inexpensive gift to lift their day.

We want to help the poor and plan to take a stand for community improvement. We intend to write our congressman.

We think about the lonely....

We are going to surprise our family with a new recipe, but just for today we will buy one more box of pre-dipped, pre-frozen, pre-cooked, pre-digested additives.

We plan to take that big trip as soon as we "get everything taken care of."

We *plan, hope,* and *intend* to be fully happy, but we rarely ever find our happiness today. Why? Why do we allow things and circumstances to rob us continually of today's happiness?

Two good reasons why we postpone our happiness are:

1. We fail to seize our moment.
2. We fail to help other people seize their moment.

Let's take a look at seizing the moment for ourselves. We will begin by going back to Jesus' words on this subject, which instruct us, "Don't be anxious about tomorrow."

God's wisdom for His people is never foolhearted. He never says, "Go out, go into debt, and spend like there's no tomorrow. Relax all morals, and chase every brainstorm." But God tells those of us who keep promising ourselves we will live tomorrow that we should never plan away our today based on a future dream.

I learned more from my father about the rewards of "seizing" the moment than from any other person in my life. He missed very few opportunities to be happy. If he got an idea, he did it immediately. On a moment's notice, he would load all eight children in a car he had just purchased and head out for somewhere. If we were in school, Mother simply notified the teacher. If one of us had a cast on, we limped along with the others. If someone had poison ivy, he or she suffered. When my father saw a chance for happiness, he seized it because he was a man of action.

Although he could have afforded to buy anything he wanted for himself, his clothes were modest, he ate simple foods, his friends were down-to-earth people, and he lived in total possession of his material gains. He was fully unimpressed by and liberated from things. Cars were made to transport people, not to save for collectors. Homes were made to live in, not to stand as a showpiece for visitors. Money was made to be spent and shared with others. All his long, prosperous life, my father used "things" to make people happy—from his family to total strangers. "Things" served my father.

Does this sound familiar to you, or do you resist such spontaneity because it is "irresponsible?" Are you one of life's great planners, always "going to" but never doing? What big thing or little gesture have you been planning for years, but it has just never been the perfect moment?

Years ago I decided that at least once a year I would write a letter to my parents and tell them something specific that I especially appreciated about them. I usually sent this at Christmas or Easter inside my card, even if I was going home. In retrospect, I'm glad I acted out my decision because the day came when that particular opportunity ceased with my father's death.

Some of my greatest natural pleasures have come from seizing little moments like sending cards, calling, and writing letters—simply inexpensive efforts at breaking monotony.

When Paul was in graduate school and we could not afford over $5.00 for entertainment, we would pop a big bag of corn and take the children to the movie on Monday evening "dollar night." It was like a breath of fresh air away from the pressure of studies. Life is filled with inexpensive pleasures, but we let routine and postponement kill most of them.

One way to stop postponing happiness is to do everything you possibly can *today* to be happy. The second way you can stop postponing happiness is to help other people seize their moment for a bit of pleasure. Get in the habit of helping others achieve their little dreams.

Jesus said the whole Book of Life can be summed up in this central theme: "Love the Lord thy God with all thy heart, and with all thy soul, and with all thy mind, and with all thy strength. Thou shalt love thy neighbor as thyself" (Mark 12:30-31).

You will never find happiness in this life if you are "too busy" or "too stingy" to help someone else get something he desires.

Years ago, before any member of my family had ever gone abroad, I got a brainstorm to see the Holy Land. I prayed, read about it, and planned. When the pressure of desire had reached explosion level, I set aside my fears and asked my parents for the money. To my utter amazement, they said, "Yes!" Evidently, they had planned on giving a special gift to all the girls that year.

My life is still rich today from that tour I took with one of the world's finest Biblical archaeologists. But it took my parents to help me fulfill my desire. This kind of generosity was typical of my parents, who had helped hundreds of people during their lifetime.

When my father died, more than a thousand people came to call on us. Business executives flew in from various parts of the country, and mentally retarded farmhands who had been given a chance to work came to show their respect. Each person told us of a time when my father had helped him seize his moment of happiness.

For the past two years, Paul and other members of our family have gone to one of the communist Eastern

Bloc nations to speak and encourage the churches. As an added treat, I always load a special suitcase full of sheets, towels, soaps, clothes, toys, chewing gum, and stacks of chocolate candy. I envision and enjoy every single bite of that candy. It tastes more delicious in their mouth than mine. Availability has dulled my tastebuds, but theirs are ripe and waiting.

Every item shared turns into happiness for the giver.

Some of you are depressed, lonely, nervous, afraid, unfulfilled, and bitter.

Stop mourning!

Stop brooding!

Stop postponing and start living. Get rid of the attitude that keeps saying, "Wait until tomorrow."

Take today's opportunity for yourself today, and help others seize their moment of happiness.

Make a promise to yourself. Say out loud, "I will stop postponing happiness for myself and for others. I will fully live every opportunity God offers me."

What mental and emotional renewal will come as you release your attitude to possess your possessions!

7

Anger and Depression

In this chapter I will discuss renewing your mind in the area of anger and depression. This type of anger is not the emotional state that is hostile and inflamed with rage. It is neither the explosive husband who beats his wife or commits criminal acts nor the person who abuses children. Such a distinct emotional portrait needs its own chapter.

Nagging, seething disappointment grinds ulcers into our stomachs and causes us to resent life instead of renewing ourselves to its possibilities. This kind of anger is much more common than rage.

Anger is the mother of depression. Repressed anger is a fertile seedbed for various forms of mental and emotional disturbances. Seething imaginations can produce chronic anxiety—one recurring, miserable feeling about something that should have been buried long ago. Anxiety can disrupt digestion, interfere with heart rhythm, cause skin rashes, and make a person feel generally miserable.

A common truism I often state is this: "Miserable people make people miserable."

Angry people are miserable, and miserable people stir up trouble. It may be trouble as simple as gossip. Or it may be as radical as the man who jumped out of his car screaming, leaving his two young children to crawl out into the middle of heavy traffic—simply because Paul and I unintentionally pulled ahead of him on the expressway!

Anger is as common as grass yet as deadly as a bullet. In reflecting back over my own battles with sickness, I realize that my digestive problems were closely linked to anger-produced, internal pressure. I was angry at ignorant people who failed to appreciate my abilities. I wanted to show people who rejected me that I could do it. I disliked pushy personalities, and I could not stand executives. In short, I seethed over any person or statement that disagreed with my position.

One day while talking with the gastroenterologist I frequently visited, he said to me, "Mona, when you have an attack with your stomach, don't worry so much about what you are eating but what is eating you!"

God's prescription for people with pent-up anger—which is most of humanity, to one degree or another—is this: "Put off ... the former conversation the old man... And be renewed in the spirit of your mind" (Ephesians 4:22-23).

What is Paul talking about when he says, "Be renewed in the spirit of your mind"? What is it about our minds that we are supposed to change?

Certainly most people cannot make drastic changes in their lifestyle. They will have to remain in the same house, with the same family, at the same job, and with the same problems. How can we possibly be "renewed" in the same old circumstances?

Fortunately, God never gives prescriptions that are impossible to swallow. When Paul wrote, "Be renewed in the spirit of your mind," he was speaking about your *attitude*. Your mind can be reformed in its attitude. Your attitude toward circumstances makes all the difference in the world in the level of happiness you maintain during the difficulties of daily life.

Every person alive gets angry. It is normal to dislike situations to the point of emotional involvement. Nothing is wrong with anger as long as it is moderate and under control. But it is sin—emotional, physical, and spiritual violation—to *retain* anger and make it a subject of prolonged meditation.

God says, "Be ye angry, and sin not" (Ephesians 4:26). That means do not grind over and over in your mind any disagreeable person or subject.

"Let not the sun go down upon your wrath" (Ephesians 4:26). This is God's limit for any situation. If you want to stay healthy, then end your anger by sundown.

People frequently come to me with concern about seemingly unprovoked "wild thoughts" that pop up in their mind. I always try to assure them that it is not the thought that produces the problem, but *what we do* with the thought once it has pushed its way into our peaceful domain.

Wild thoughts and anger quite often find more expression in people who are suffering some type of phys-

85

ical illness. Explosions and implosions are common during periods of confinement. Anytime the body feels weak or incapable of independent action, the mind panics and resorts to anger, which soon becomes depression.

Men especially find it difficult to be confined. We often counsel young people who refer to a period when their father was confined at home as a painful time in their life. Many of them carry deep wounds as a result of seeing violent outbursts of masculine frustration.

A young girl with a nervous twitch came to us one evening. "I feel like I am falling apart," she said. As we began to minister, one of the first scars exposed was her inability to forgive her father for the cruel way he treated his family when he was out of work. The wrong attitude during confinement is deadly.

We recently visited a new friend in a state correctional institution. As we sat chatting with him, I said, "Look, if you really want to, you can use this time of confinement to set yourself free on the inside. It can be a time of getting your case together. You have the time now to learn all about God and let Him teach you all about yourself—and why He has put you on this earth."

The right attitude during any confinement will bring you into a better mental state than before. The wrong attitude will build into erratic explosions. It all depends on your attitude.

DEPRESSION IN WOMEN

I watched a psychologist on TV discuss women who are bound by the modern definition of beauty. They feel they must be pencil thin in order to look good. "Some women are depressed simply because they do not have enough good food to eat," he said.

Millions of women, who have been brainwashed into achieving the perfect size-ten figure, drink one-calorie liquids and eat a minimum of nutritious food. Then they wonder why they feel jittery. The nervous system operates on food energy. Smart people will take their personal build into account, along with the amount of energy they are required to expend during a day, *before* they establish a "normal" weight size for themselves.

I would rather work than eat. Sometimes when I feel excessively tired over a period of days, I stop and ask myself, "How much food am I actually consuming?" Invariably I find that I am eating only one good meal with a nutritious snack to supplement a long day's work. That is when I stop everything and take time to treat my body right.

You cannot expect your car to operate to its maximum if you put cheap gas in it and never take it for necessary tune-ups. Depression is certain to follow junk food and too few quality calories. While I am not hung-up on any Eastern-inspired health cuisine, I have gone back to my delicious, rural American way of eating plenty of fruits and vegetables, good grains, nuts, and reasonable portions of various meats. The brain needs quality fuel if it is to function at maximum level.

A woman recently came up to me after a meeting with a common depression that arose from another source. She was in the menopausal stage of her life. Hormones, or lack of them, can produce strange sensations. Sometimes you feel as though your body is about to shut down; and sometimes you think it is going to blast off! What I advised this lady is the same good word I want to pass on to any person whose depression is physically produced:

"Your spirit does not have hormones and is not subject to physical ups and downs. It is subject only to its diet of spiritual nutrition. Feed your spirit God's Word and godly fellowship, and your spirit will carry your body along until your physical situation balances out. Never let your body dictate the course of your day. Tell your body what your plans are and force it to follow directions—and keep busy."

If I permit it, my body cops out of almost every worthwhile project I undertake. But I *refuse* to miss the joy of living simply because I have a fragile make-up. I have learned to discipline my body for the best interest of my overall welfare. My life is exciting, and I am no longer bloated with anger or battling depression.

ANGER—THE HIDDEN CULPRIT

Excluding the legitimate physical possibilities, however, *anger* is the culprit that produces depression in the majority of us. Life disappoints us. We don't or we can't do anything to change the situation, so we put the hurt on the back burner of our mind and start the pot simmering. Each day we take our repressed anger and stir it several times with thoughts. Anger can stay alive only as long as we feed it thoughts. In fact, when God was instructing me about how to deal with anger, He brought the following illustration to my mind:

Just imagine you have a little pet named Anger. Each night you put your pet in a nice, clean cage, with its well-attended food and water bowl. (That means your last thoughts at night are troubled.) Each morning you run to the cage to let Anger out. You gently pick up the prickly bundle of trouble and place it on your shoulder. Then whoever comes across your path that day must deal with both you and your pet, Anger!

What would happen, on the other hand, if you did not want anger in your life any longer? How could you get rid of it? Let's say anger is a life-threatening, poisonous creature that needs to be annihilated. What would you do? Step on it, throw away the cage, and forget about it, of course. How simple! That solution became completely obvious to me when my internal war ended. You and I can be liberated from the anger and depression we no longer want to carry.

Thoughts fuel anger. Your thoughts keep anger alive. It is not your *circumstances* but your *thoughts* that provide the food for your present attitude.

How many of you are harboring anger at someone or something today? Has your anger helped the situation? I am not talking about some brief rise in emotion, I am talking about prolonged anger. Has your anger helped the situation? Has your anger grown with time? Has your anger brought you *closer to* or taken you *further from* God during this situation?

Remember, when I say anger, I am also referring to resentment and disappointment. It is difficult to separate these two emotional responses from anger. Disappointment and resentment will often take on the characteristics of anger and actually produce the same feelings of depression inside you.

You may be saying, "I don't deserve to be stuck with the job I have; I got a raw deal from life!" This may be absolutely true. But God has taught me a beautiful thing about attitude: wrong thoughts on my part, regardless of the element of truth in them, will hold back the joy of living from me. *Anger and resentment will do nothing for us but delay God's intervention into our situation.*

Although you may have every natural right in the world to be angry—you may explain your case to a hundred people, and they may all agree that you are right— the truth remains: angry people are unhappy people.

Peace of mind and happiness simply do not live in an attitude of anger. Learning to deal with anger will eliminate a great portion of depression from your life.

In this chapter, I have selected three areas where people harbor anger. These three categories need continual mental attention and renewal. If you will bring them out into the open, identify them, admit to any hostility, you will find relief for your emotions.

UNFORGIVENESS

I often hear these words from hostile people: "I cannot forgive them." I have confessed it in the past, and I am sure you have, too. But now we are going to deal with it.

Say with me, out loud if possible, "With God all things are possible. It is possible for me to forgive. I can forgive that person." Now I want you to envision the person or situations that you hold anger toward and say, "Father God, forgive me for holding anger against _____. I forgive _____, and I release all anger against them."

MARRIAGE

Now, let us go to the second area of conflict that produces seething hostility within us. This area of anger prompts many people to make this statement: "My marriage is terrible!"

God showed me something beautiful about this situation. He showed me that no marriage is terrible—they only contain some terribly frustrated people.

Marriage is an honorable estate created by God. It is a beautiful, holy, and satisfying union. We need to stop making verbal attacks against this sacred institution. Early one morning, I awakened with a book on my mind. I was writing *A Statement On Sex—Loud and Clear*. As I was meditating on the last chapter, I said, "Lord, why did you create sex? That seems like such a strange thing for you to have included in the procreation of life!"

For the next two hours, God took me through various portions of the Bible. He showed me that the husband-wife union is the most graphic statement He has made to mankind concerning their *spiritual* union with their Creator. God showed me that His jealous love over us is best understood by the careful heart a husband and wife hold for each other as they watch over the sanctity of their intimacy. Absolutely no other lovers are permitted and no other affection is welcome.

The ultimate wound to the heart comes from betrayed love. The greatest spiritual union on earth is between God and His spiritual son or daughter. The greatest natural union on earth is between a husband and wife. These two unions should never be perverted or violated.

Marriage is honorable. *Your* marriage is honorable. God's Word says, "Husbands, love your wives, and be not bitter against them" (Colossians 3:19). That is, do not be harsh, hateful, unkind, cruel, or abusive.

The Word also says, "Wives, submit yourselves unto your own husbands, as it is fit in the Lord" (Colossians 3:18).

The word *submit* means to "subordinate" yourself to his leadership. A wife rules best under the protection of her husband. A home works best where the man assumes his responsibility as leader under God, while the woman assumes her role as leader under her godly husband.

Obviously, a wife does not submit to sin on the part of the husband. As the Word states clearly, she is to subordinate *as it is fit*—proper—in the Lord. But a "protected" ruler can afford to build more wisely when she does not have to concern herself with also being the porter at the door. Male leadership in the family is emotionally healthy for both men and women. I believe the innate desire of every man is to defend and protect his property, while the woman has a natural desire to be the one shielded.

In spite of some extreme feminist thrusts to burst rocks and operate cranes, I believe most women still enjoy the comfortable feeling of masculine protection.

The institution of marriage is solid, but you and your partner may have slipped off its foundation. Your husband or wife may not be responsible or godly. You may have been terribly wounded in life by them. If so, would you take the first step toward healing and turn over that deep scar to the healing work of Jesus by releasing the anger you hold toward him or her? In spite of the deadness you may be experiencing this very moment, would you say, "Father, I forgive my (wife, husband)_____. I release the anger I have been harboring against them. I ask You to send good into their lives and restore them as a person."

Some of you may even need to admit that you have a "death wish" against your partner. This is often the case. You imagine that your life would be good if only your partner would die and get out of the way. Obviously, such a thought is not only lethal to your marriage but it will invite a terrible fear of death into your own mind.

If you have a "death wish" against any person, I want to encourage you to take it to God right now. Confess your sin, and evict such a notion with all its accompanying fears from your mind.

EMPLOYMENT

Finally, I want to deal with an area of anger that prompts millions to make this statement: "I hate my work."

I must confess that as an adult I have never hated my work. Ever since I left the cotton fields of Alabama, I have always found great pleasure in what I do. I enjoy housework, and I enjoy cooking. I enjoyed art as a profession for ten years. I enjoy writing and teaching God's Word. I enjoy work! It gives me great enthusiasm for each day of living. I am continually setting goals for myself and planning projects of outreach to help other people. Work makes life exciting.

At one period of my life, I was hardly able to do any work at all. With a complete physical breakdown complicated by an emotional crash landing, I knew what it meant to be too weak and too afraid to participate in anything productive. That is one reason I am so grateful to be alive and happy today.

Whenever I am tired and feeling sorry for myself now, I just remember those miserable old days and start thanking God for giving me strength to scrub dishes, do laundry, baby-sit my grandchildren, and write—all at the same time!

Whatever you do, do it unto the Lord and not unto man. That way your labor will not be in vain in the Lord. (See 1 Corinthians 15:58.)

Many people hate their work because they feel "unappreciated." In fact, I read an article in which surveyors asked thousands of employees what they desired most from their employer. The first general agreement was "appreciation." We human beings have a great emotional need to be appreciated. But more often than not, we are taken for granted.

You may think that people in Christian work would get encouragement from every direction. Not so. In fact, if you cannot take criticism, don't go into the ministry.

For example, just this week a sweet little lady came to me with a message from someone wanting to know if I had gotten rid of the "spirit of Jezebel" yet!

I learned some time ago not to do my work for the praise and recognition of people. It is simply too disappointing. The boss may not appreciate your extra efforts, and the people you work with may not appreciate your extra mile—but God does. If you dedicate your day to Him in all that you do and carry gratitude in your heart all day, the Lord will delight Himself in your production. He will reward you with great peace of mind and happiness.

I know this because I do it all the time. You can be happy at work in spite of your circumstances. All you have to do is say as you go to work, "Lord, I thank You for my job. Thank You for the health and skill to do my work well. Thank You for the money it provides for me and my family. I dedicate my job to You, Lord. I will not complain about work from this day forward."

Anger and hostility toward your work will drain away as you confess these liberating expressions of gratitude. You will find yourself with a lot more energy for doing the things you must. Gratitude does wonders for your attitude. Your attitude will do wonders for your happiness quotient. Happiness will do wonders for your health.
- A healthy body....
- A healthy marriage....
- A healthy work situation—

and anger and depression will find it hard to make themselves at home with your emotions.

You were created to be useful. Whether you are young and just beginning, middle-aged and fighting the competition, or retired and shifting to a different pace, you have something to offer the human race. You are a person who is needed. Invest yourself where you are and be grateful. Never give anger a chance to rob you of even one priceless day of life on this wonderful planet.

8

Fear

Imagine you saw a man holding a beautiful, expensive fishing rod with a silver hook on the end of the line; and he said to you, "I'm going to catch a prize marlin on this hook." If he then made a grand throw into the middle of a football field, what would you think?

"That person is insane! You can't catch fish on land!" you would say.

And that is true. If you want a specific thing, you must go where it is and do whatever is necessary to obtain it. This truth applies also in the realm of emotional stability. You cannot cast out fear and catch confidence anywhere but in the place where real confidence may be found.

After many years of struggling with fear, I have found that place of dependable confidence. I want to share with you a place you can go to throw away your fears and learn to live with the assurance you need.

I was raised to be self-confident. My parents instilled great courage into each of their eight children. Not one of us thought the world was too big to conquer. We were assured that we could do anything any other person could accomplish.

From grade one to college, I was among the first to volunteer for whatever challenge was presented. It simply never occurred to me that I might possibly fail. My senior class in high school awarded me so many honors that the teachers said it was unfair and gave some of the titles to other students.

In college, I made the dean's list, was a leader in my church, sang in the choir, spoke often at various functions, and had my finger in just about every available pie. But one day, like a bolt of lightening, fear hit my mind.

Almost without warning, I suddenly became afraid of everything and everybody. Normal routine seemed impossible to accomplish, and the things I had always enjoyed I now hated. A simple routine such as going out among people put a band around my throat like a choker. I was afraid to go to the shopping center for fear of getting trapped. I had a horror of standing in front of people with every eye centered on what I was doing. I shied away from small, intimate groups—they were too personal. I became obsessed with the fear of dying. I was afraid to be left alone for five minutes. In a word, I became afraid of fear itself. Fear—just the thought of that word made me panic.

This was the beginning of my quest for real, unfailing confidence. It took me only a few weeks to realize that courage built on personality, name, talent, or public speaking courses is fragile and can wash out from under you on a moment's notice.

Honors fade, superstars slip, money can be lost, and positions are passed on to someone younger or better qualified. Even degrees yellow with age and must be continually updated. When this happens, what kind of confidence will you be left with?

In my own experience, I learned that self-confidence can be wounded or even shattered beyond repair. But I also discovered a confidence that is not subject to natural circumstances. In the first few weeks of my nervous collapse, I tried the mental approach: positive thinking, psychiatry, good books, music, and long walks in nature.

These provided temporary relief, but each step forward was always accompanied by a big slide backward. Sooner or later, the old fears would rise up again, and I would find myself shaking all over, trying to grab hold of something. Many of you know exactly what I am talking about.

Gradually my natural props were abandoned one by one; and I finally turned to God with all my heart, mind, will, and emotion. He took me "one day at a time" and taught me how to rely on Him and His Word when I was alone. He showed me how to depend on Him when my body felt strange—my head dizzy—my heart palpitating—my breathing laborious. He taught me how to lean on Him when I stood up to speak. He taught me how to get control of my mind when phobic thoughts said, "You can't go into that crowd of people!"

God's healing prescription is found in Proverbs 14:26: "In the fear of the Lord is strong confidence: and his children shall have a place of refuge."

FALSE FEAR

In a recent documentary, behavioral scientists observed the reaction of gorillas to a fake leopard. The scientists had stuffed a leopard skin and placed it in the habitat of the gorillas. Although the leopard did not move, the gorillas were screaming, running, jumping, and warning each other of impending doom.

However false, that leopard posed a threat in the minds of the fear-filled gorillas. It took only one gorilla to spot the leopard and send the signal, and the whole group was seized with panic.

How typical of fear. Fear strikes panic in every living creature. As I continued to watch the documentary, I noticed a female gorilla run by; and I received an important message. The only calm animal in the entire frenzy clung to that mother—it was her baby!

Seemingly without a care in the world, that baby gorilla had its eyes set squarely on its mother's face and its arms around her strong shoulders. During that scene I began to realize a truth for my own emotional stability.

The baby gorilla felt secure in the middle of all that hysteria because its safety did not depend on circumstances. To the baby ape, circumstances meant absolutely nothing as long as its strong protector was there. A *"person,"* not a situation, was that baby's security. Regardless of what happened, as long as its mother was touchable, the baby held on.

For those of you who remember your children when they were newborn infants, you may recall how they never took their eyes off you. Whether bathing, eating, or lying in a crib, they followed you wherever you went.

By instinct they sensed security in a familiar person. That is the foundation of confidence—a person.

Do you have a fearful imagination? Are you frequently threatened by imaginary enemies—car accidents, plane crashes, every new disease that comes out of the obituary column, all the old diseases that did not get you the first time around, food poisoning, or fear of eating? Several years ago, a woman died from botulism—food poisoning from eating improperly canned tuna. It was the first case we had ever heard of. I still have trouble eating tuna! I go ahead, pray over it, and then eat, but that incident is often there to remind me. Tremendous power lies in one single suggestion.

Many people have a fear of crowds. "A lot of people will be there tonight," they say, and their fearful thoughts tell them not to get into that crowd because something will happen.

We have all kinds of phobias: fear of leaving home, fear of driving, fear of close places, etc. There is even a fear of fire. How many times have you prepared to leave home when an inner urging said to you, "What if the house burns while you are gone?" All these and many more "enemies" travel through life with us, robbing us of the confidence we need to remain emotionally stable.

Some people have pyromania, and they go around lighting fires. I recently met a young man sentenced to twenty-five years in prison for burning buildings in Boston. A spirit exists behind pyromania, and it is a power that incites fear of fire in other people.

If you have a problem with fear, then you need to learn the lesson of the baby gorilla. You need to learn to put your trust in a dependable Person. Instead of look-ing at vacillating circumstances, put your trust in one de-pending, unchanging factor—the Lord Jesus Christ.

WHEN FEAR STRIKES

In Romans 8:15, we read these words of direction: "For ye have not received the spirit of bondage again to fear." If you are reading this book and have received Jesus into your life to be your *Lord,* you did not receive a spirit of fearful bondage along with Jesus. Fear is a bondage. Fear does not belong to the Christian's peace of mind. "But ye have received the Spirit of adoption, whereby we cry, Abba, Father" (Romans 8:15).

The spirit mentioned here is the Holy Spirit. The mo-ment the Holy Spirit adopted you to God, you were no longer an orphan. Spiritual orphans panic, but you are no longer an orphan. You are not a prey to the enemy or the circumstances around you. You have a Father to hold on to when the enemy threatens. The Holy Spirit has adopted you to God. This truth is established throughout the New Testament. Therefore, when you or the people around you become afraid, you can hold on to your Father and leave the screaming to the unbe-lievers.

In 1 Corinthians 2:12, God says Christians have not received the *spirit of the world,* which is *fear;* but believ-ers have received the Spirit of God. Fear is the spirit of the world. Do you know that? Let me repeat it. *Fear is the spirit of the world!* If you have fear thoughts, you are letting the spirit of the world occupy your mind. As a Christian, you have been adopted by the Holy Spirit of

God and should not listen to the spirit of the world. That is why God told us that we would be kept in perfect peace if we keep our mind on Him. I assure you, that is the only situation I have found that will keep me in peace during a stressful situation.

In Montreal one evening, I sat on board a plane that was completely fogged in. I was traveling alone. The plane slowly began to taxi toward the runway, then it turned around and went back into the terminal. The captain's voice finally announced, "Ladies and gentleman, the visibility will not permit take off at present. We will assist those of you who have connecting flights as much as possible."

Hardly five minutes later, with fog rolling in billows around us and the terminal barely visible, we began to back out a second time. Assisted by official trucks, the plane crept down the runway until we got the signal to fasten our seat belts. Then, in the misty blur of blue illumination, those big engines began to whine, and through the fog we went!

What was I doing? I looked up toward heaven and said, "Father, I am on your mission. I ask you to look down through this fog and guide those pilots by your supernatural wisdom." I praised and thanked the Lord for His faithfulness, and I went calmly through that hour of indecision with the supernatural peace of God around me.

What do you do when fear strikes? What is the *first* thing you should do?

Speak the name of Jesus. Speak the words of Jesus. Praise your Eternal Father, and sooner or later your fake leopard will be exposed for what it is.

This is exactly what happened to those foolish gorillas. After a grand demonstration of fear, it slowly began to dawn on the apes to check out their enemy—perhaps he was not so lethal after all.

One by one, inch by inch, they sneaked up to the stuffed animal. Ultimately they were standing face to face with him. One reached out and touched his back. When there was no threat, they began to smack the fake enemy right and left. What a party they held—victory over the enemy!

You do have a real enemy. I am not trying to minimize him. You have many natural enemies in this life, but you will doubtless meet more false threats than actual confrontations. A line from a play I once saw has stuck in my mind for several years: "A coward dies a thousand deaths, but a brave man only once."

Real enemies or fake, circumstances are not the criteria for your confidence. There is a Person you can turn to for help.

Is it true? Can God really show you a hiding place in the midst of people and fearful circumstances? Oh, yes. How do I know this?

1. God says it!
2. I have personally experienced it!

Self-confidence is weak. It is fragile, unstable, and entirely dependent on physical stability.

OUR STRONG CONFIDENCE
If your health were excellent, your home paid for, and your business progressing; if you had lovely children and

a wonderful marriage; if there were no wars, a stable economy, and good weather ... if *everything* in your natural life could always be perfect, you might be able to make it with self-confidence—until you reached the end of your life. But God-confidence works any time and every time. God-confidence makes cowards stand in control of their fears and runaway thoughts submit to reason. Confidence in God causes mental confusion to line up with His sensible order.

A great big football player I know feels as though he has a band around his neck whenever he gets into a crowd of people. Performers continually admit to taking tranquilizers before they go on stage. People come to us petrified at the possibility of a job interview.

But do you want to know one of the things God taught me that will help you in this situation? Never look at people as a group. Each person is an individual. Just as you cope with your problems one day at a time, you can approach people one at a time. A group may pose a threat to you, but one at a time you can handle them.

Beyond this, however, when I am confronted with people, I depend on God-confidence to carry me through the situation. If I am in a big crowd—say New York City—at three in the afternoon and I'm getting onto a bus or subway, I mentally block out all those people by putting my thoughts on Jesus.

Out of my spirit, I silently begin talking to Him. I worship. I praise. I pray. I refresh my mind with His words and even hum a song if I feel like it until I have complete control of my emotions. And it has never failed to work beautifully for me.

It will take time to develop this relationship with the Father so that you can practice His presence wherever you are. But it is going to take time for you to get a handle on yourself anyway. Why not adopt God's *infallible* plan?

If you have lost confidence in yourself, it is possible to regain your stability and be better off than before. I am. I know I am not Superwoman. I never have to pretend that I am again. Naturally speaking, I am fragile and subject to failure. But spiritually, I am as stable and dependable as the One who will not fail me. I have discovered solid confidence. He simply will not let me be emotionally destroyed.

Please say out loud with me now:

- I can regain my confidence.
- I do not have to be afraid of people.
- I am free to go wherever I choose.
- I can and will meet my responsibilities.
- Right now I cast all my fears onto Jesus,
  and I receive His strong confidence.

Now then, every time you feel afraid—in the middle of the night; talking to your boss; applying for a job; speaking before a group of people; entertaining people in your home; feeling weak, dizzy, or shaky—I want you to refresh yourself with this healing promise:

"In the fear of the Lord is strong confidence; and his children shall have a place of refuge" (Proverbs 14:26). Then pray, "Thank You, Father, in Jesus' Name, for confidence. I look to You and depend on You. I lean on You. Thank You for strong confidence."

This spiritual prescription can be taken as often as needed for as long as the problem arises. It will eventually cast out your fears and renovate your way of looking at threatening situations.

Now get up, go out, and put faith into action!

9

Grief or Peace

Some of you may be surprised to learn that the biblical definition of the word "heart" covers much more than feelings or emotion. The original Greek and Hebrew definition of the term "heart" includes mind, will, and emotion. Therefore, when the Bible says, "Let the peace of God rule in your hearts" (Colossians 3:15), it means that we are to let the peace of God rule in our mind, our will, and our emotion.

The Word says to let (permit, allow) the peace of God rule. This means that you and I have an active part to play in bringing about good emotional health in our lives.

Life is never perfect. We need to understand that. Life will never run smoothly at all times. Change, disappointment, death, natural disasters, crime, poverty, job loss, divorce, transfers, child-parent conflicts—everyone's life contains undertows from time to time. We live in a world of change. Change threatens our peace of mind. It has a tendency to unbalance our mental equilibrium. But God has peace, confidence, and assurance for us that is not subject to natural circumstances.

In order to maintain your emotional balance, you must have a standard. If everything around you is changing, your thoughts must have an anchor that is not going to shift with the current. Whether or not we admit it, life holds some absolutes. My mind was filled with knowledge when I became unstable. But knowing God and allowing His thoughts (the Bible) to renovate my natural attitude has given me peace of mind far beyond natural circumstances.

A difference lies between God's peace and the world's definition of it. The peace of God surpasses all natural understanding simply because His peace is not dependent on natural circumstances. Neither is God's peace dependent on any person in your life.

The circumstances of life can be very unsettling. I want to help you understand that, although you may be cut adrift, you can be anchored even while you are being unsettled. It is possible to retain mental calmness even when you see everything around you crashing to the ground.

Good businesses fail; good families fall apart; good talents go unrecognized; and good dreams shatter all around you. But if your confidence is based on God, you will take refuge in His supernatural peace until the storm passes.

We confront a lot of enemies to our peace of mind because we live in a fallible world. We meet a lot of enemies through our thoughts, our conversations, our choice of friends, the places we go, the books we read, and the public media. In this chapter I want to discuss an enemy that each of us must face at some time in our life. It can be the most shattering of all, if we allow it. This common enemy is called *grief.*

Grief is a hurt or wound that comes from loss. Death, divorce, separation, disagreement, job politics—whatever brings loss into your life invariably brings grief.

Stop and think for a minute. How much time do you spend thinking about things that cannot possibly be changed? We have been programmed by natural morbidity to think that we care only if we grieve. "You don't care," people accuse us, "if you don't grieve." We think and talk grief, and others talk grief to us. Most television programs would have little subject matter if they removed excessive grief from their plot. Never mind normal grief; nothing portrays hopelessness as well as the camera. In living color, news reporters and superstars encourage grief-stricken people to remain hopeless each night.

If you are suffering from the loss of a person, a friendship, or a position in life, you may choose one of three directions: *withdrawal, defense,* or *face-up.* You may *withdraw* from people and give yourself totally to grief and remorse. This will make you miserable. Or you may *defend* yourself with, "Why me?" An overblown case of self-pity will cause you to develop a defensive attitude toward the world and lash out at everybody and everything that attempts to draw you out of your misery. Finally, you may *face the situation* and do what is necessary to return to emotional peace and productive living.

Every person alive has lost something or someone at some time in their life. You may be in the eye of the storm right now, groping and grasping to find your way. If so, I want to help you cope with your loss. And the best way I know is to face up to the truth.

Step number one in facing your loss is to *admit that there has been a change.* It does no good to pretend to yourself and everyone around you that nothing has changed. Do not try any longer to keep everything as it was. Pretending will only hurt you. If you have suffered loss, things in your life will be different. No one person or position in life can be an eternal institution that lasts unaltered forever. Every time we lose someone or something close to us we are hit with this reality—nothing on this earth is permanent.

Only spiritual realities are unshakable. Everything and everyone else including you and I will undergo drastic changes. But do not despair! Change is not the end of the line. Change does not mean cessation. Change can even open new doors you never thought possible.

When my father died, my mother was at a loss. Not only was there a great unexpected financial shake-up, but my mother was now forced to manage everything herself—do house repairs, pay car insurance, buy new tires, etc.

When the reality of this change dawned on my mother, she began to age. When she came for a visit, she just sat in her chair. Whereas before she used to enter into conversation, she now remained silent. Her favorite pastime had always been shopping, but now it made no difference if we looked through the big malls or not. "We will do whatever you want," she would respond.

Seeing my mother so obviously unhappy moved me to take her situation to the only One who could possibly help. "Father," I said, "You know my mother has been a faithful daughter and a pillar in that little Methodist church. She's been the greatest mother, neighbor, and community person she could possibly be. She has literally poured out her life for her family, her community, and Your Church. Lord, I am asking You to reward her by making her last days the best. Do whatever is necessary, but make her happy all the days of her life."

I prayed these words repeatedly over the next few months. Finally, to our utter amazement, a member of the family called and said, "Guess what? Mother has a new friend!"

This was news. One thing my mother never showed any interest in was men—almost including my father! She had said a thousand times, "If your daddy dies first, I will never even consider looking at another man." We were convinced.

One year later, Mother, looking ten years younger than her age—smiling and happy to be alive—announced that this gentlemen she had known as a child was now going to be her new husband. That was two years ago, and grief has had no opportunity to rob her of her right to live happily every day of her life.

Has it been all roses? As far as she is concerned, yes. As for perfect communication among such a large family, no. But this is what God brought to my understanding concerning situations resulting from other people's choices.

Do you want that person you love to be genuinely happy? Or do you want them to have what *you* think will make his or her life complete? This may call for mental adjustment on your part. You may need a new way of viewing the person you wish to help.

In my case, I determined that I wanted my mother to be happy according to her definition of what she needed. Therefore, I have had peace with her joy, and I have done everything possible to help one older couple find the pleasures of companionship. I am glad to have a part in helping anyone overcome excessive grief and loss.

TAKING POSITIVE STEPS

In my own life, I have suffered numerous minor losses, but only two major changes that could never be reversed. Let me share some notes I jotted down while those losses were still fresh in my emotions.

In an effort to be honest with my feelings, immediately after losing someone I loved through death, I found that I had to walk away from grief by refusing to think about that person during the course of my day. I put away all photographs and kept my thoughts on other things.

I forced both my mind and my conversation to stay away from the departed person. My natural tendency was to run straight for him every morning when I woke up, but I disciplined my thoughts and denied grief any opportunity. In denying grief its rights, I also dealt a blow to depression.

To put the memory of the departed person aside for a few months is not cruel. You will come back to them in thought later. While the wound is fresh, keep your thoughts occupied with those people who are still around you. Go outside your home mentally and physically, and get involved in life with other people as soon as possible. Do not neglect your duties or allow yourself to withdraw even for one day from your normal routine.

As time passes and the wound from the loss is healed, then permit your thoughts to go back to the good parts of your relationship with that person. *But always keep your thoughts away from the moment of loss.*

This is something I realized during my loss; the grieving person is inclined to ignore the countless years of *good experiences* they may have shared with the departed person. They tend to think only of the moment of loss—the funeral, the flowers, the sympathy cards, and the calls. No, no! Avoid those days for a long while to come. Do not be preoccupied with death. Allow your mind to be renewed among the living.

Jesus said that whoever lives and believes in Him will never die. (See John 3:15.) God is not the God of the dead, but of the *living*. Grief, death, and loss are foreign to life. Keeping your thoughts on loss is the same as introducing foreign matter into your bloodstream—it will cause infection. Do not infect your mind with infectious thoughts of death!

Perhaps your loss is not a person but instead a position or possessions. Many people have committed suicide over such losses. A career starts downhill; a family fortune is lost; embarrassment sets in; grief mixes with anger and hostility; and you fall apart emotionally— body, mind, and spirit.

If this has happened to you, then you must use the same discipline as the grieving person we just described. Whatever thing (or things) you may have had snatched from your hands is *gone*. Don't look back with all those mental "if onlys." There is no need to spend your time dreaming backward. It is gone. In fact, it will help you to say to yourself, "That position I held is gone. I release myself completely from it. It is a past experience!"

Having told yourself the truth, let me suggest the next step to take. *Forget the past and get on with the business of living.* What I am telling you is precisely what I have done both in the death situation and in the loss of a position.

When my father died, what should have been a handsome inheritance for his eight children was put on an auction block (literally) and sold to the highest bidder. Because of the family's prosperity, everybody for hundreds of miles around knew of the collapse. Out of jealousy many applauded, while friends were sincerely sorry. In any event, the family was suddenly faced with great changes and adjustment problems. Some were embarrassed, and others were incensed. Still others grew numb from the daily news of another domino collapsing.

As the months went by, most of us made the necessary adjustments. Given time, life has great healing in it. Our mother married again, and one sister went on to complete her doctorate and is well-positioned on the staff of a fine university. One brother went into the music industry as a gospel singer, and another brother went to the Midwest and started his own oil business. Others went into the insurance business, and so on.

Were we grieved? Yes. But we did not allow ourselves to remain among our losses. Instead, we got up and forced ourselves back out among the living.

Too many people live their lives meshed into the life of another person, a career, a job, or a business. That is dangerous planning. Grief is quick to take advantage of such people.

A young friend of ours went through a sizable identity crisis because she lived as though her husband were the only important person in the family. While it is right to honor your partner and give him or her due respect, each of us is an individual. And each of us has an individual purpose for living on this earth.

If you know God has placed you on this earth for a specific purpose that only you can fulfill, then you will be better able to realize that you have a divine responsibility to live every day of your life.

You have no right to stop living! You are responsible to get up from your losses and get on with your eternal purpose for being alive. You have been given a great and priceless treasure. Life is the most valuable commodity in the entire universe, and you have your fair share of it. You have not been slighted in the least. You are the owner of a portion of life. As long as you live, you have a great responsibility to put your personal life to good use.

You are never to retire from living while you are on this earth. God simply does not excuse giving up!

Take some positive steps away from grief in the direction of renewed purpose and fulfillment today.

Say with me (out loud, if possible):

- "I am an individual."
- "I am here on this earth for a purpose."
- "My purpose is important."
- "God wants me to be alive today, and I want to be alive in this new day."
- "I have important work to do, and with the help of God I will do it!"

Now I want to pray with you:

"Father, in Jesus' Name, I ask You to seal this wonderful truth in my heart. I am important before You. I do have purpose. You want me to have Your peace, Father, and it is possible. I put my mind on You right now, and I ask You to use me to bless You and to bless people. I am forgetting the things I have lost. I am even going to commit those wonderful people I have lost to You. They are with You, Father. They are in Your care. But now, Lord, I ask You to help me turn my mind to my own responsibilities at hand, that I may run my course as those who have gone on before me; that I may find new work (if you have lost old work); that I may find new relationships (if you have lost old ones); that I may become united (if there has been divorce); and that I may become united back into life with other people. Father, I ask You to help me break out of this grievous and withdrawn situation in which I have put myself.

118

You are able to renew my heart again. I ask now for Your supernatural peace to come upon every mind praying this prayer. In Jesus' Name, I know for certain that the peace of God can sustain me even if every person and everything around me falls away. God is sufficient! Bless the Lord. Amen."

10

Spite and Revenge

We once met a person aboard a luxurious cruise ship who was going home to have a man killed. Having been cheated out of a large sum of money, this otherwise wonderful gentleman felt justice could best be served by ridding the world of one more dishonest business tycoon. Vengeance was burning in his breast.

After several days of talking with us, this angry man decided to ignite his zeal with a different fire. He abandoned his plan of revenge and committed his life to burn with the reality of the forgiving God. Each Christmas we receive a letter from this gentleman, and he is still thanking us for pointing him to a better way of living.

There is a better way of living than vengeance and a better way of thinking than spite. You can get rid of excessive emotional worries that drain your mind of good ideas, your body of useful energy, and your spirit of peace and happiness.

God tells you His prescription for emotional drain in Ephesians 4:23: "Be renewed in the spirit of your mind." That "spirit of your mind" is referring to the attitude from which you draw your thoughts. Your mind is always thinking. You cannot alter that fact. But you can change your attitude and give your thoughts a better summit from which to motivate.

What attitude continually upsets you? You can learn to draw your thoughts from a better source. God says it is possible. But you have to make the effort. In this chapter we are going to take a look at a common emotional drain called "spite": as we used to say when we were children, "I'll pay you back!"

Have you ever said to someone, "I'll get even with you"? Human nature has a drive to even the score—to settle the account. We do not like to be left holding the bag when somebody else got the goods.

On the other hand, isn't it a great feeling to go into a department store or public utility where you owe a bill and find out you don't owe as much as you thought? Perhaps it has already been paid, and they wish to return your check in full.

One spring, Paul and I gave concerts for the military in Europe. Three years later, we found out the account had not been properly settled when we received a handsome check for the balance of payment due. Christmas in September!

I want you to celebrate some good news. Your account has also been properly settled. You never have to make another payment against any person who has hurt you in any way, large or small, as long as you live. You are under no obligation to use your time, energy, or valuable life ever again to try to even the score with your enemies.

God says that vengeance is His. (See Romans 12:19.) He will repay those who do evil against you. God will pick up your bill! Isn't that good news? If someone has hurt you, all you have to do is pray for him, forgive him, be fair to him, and leave the balance due to God.

In the Psalms, David said, "The way of the ungodly shall perish" (Psalm 1:6).

Stop for a minute. Let's think about some of the ungodly people who got their account settled:

- Where is Hitler, the hater of the Jews? He suffered a disgraceful death by suicide.
- Where is Nero, the insane destroyer of Christians—dead, and a historical joke for whom people name their dog.
- Where is Lenin, the hater of God—dead, and all that is left by which to remember him is communism.
- Where is Darwin, the agnostic theologian who elevated his word above God's— dead, and his findings already in question.

Where are all the so-called great names of the past who laughed at God's moral laws? Every week I see a familiar face on a popular magazine that tells the tragic story of frustrated fame's battle with alcohol, drugs, or emotional sickness.

What about everyday people like you and me? Think of all the casualties you know personally that occurred when payday came.

I am thinking now of a man in our community who was disgracefully cruel to his family. He repeatedly gambled away their money, drank excessively, and was unfaithful to a wife who bore him fourteen children, of which one was retarded and three died at birth. Yet his wife and children did nothing to "settle the account with him" beyond a minor threat now and then. The children grew up and moved away. The wife eventually died. And that man was left to spend his last years on earth as a lonely, fearful, and blind shell of a human being.

We recently visited a young executive in the hospital who had a short time to live. For years he had used his position in life to manipulate and control the lives of other people; but when death came, he crawled up in bed like a little boy and quietly passed away.

Given time, God has arranged life so that vengeance and spite are never necessary. To prematurely administer punishment out of your own anger never draws anything but fire.

You can never force an attitude of fairness into the hearts of other people. Your spite may cause them to agree outwardly, but their spirit of injustice will find other ways of retaliation. That is why "getting even" is so futile. You become a slave to an attitude that is always having to balance the scorecard.

A couple came to us one evening with a tremendous story of spite—its effects and cure. Briefly stated, the woman had an adulterous relationship with another man. Her husband found out and paid her back by having an affair with another woman. Their children then proceeded to pay them both back by going wild on drugs, alcohol, and sexual unrestraint. The result was complete family disintegration.

The cure came when the woman met the true and eternal Lover of her soul, Jesus. She introduced her husband to the Great Forgiver of sins. He was set free and forgave his wife as well. The children followed suit by forgiving their parents and receiving their own forgiveness. When we met this family, they were kneeling together around the altar dedicating their lives to greater commitment to God and each other.

The cause of disintegration: spite.

The cure for sin and resulting wounds: forgiveness.

Some men would never have forgiven that wife. Some children would never have forgiven their parents. But what beautiful healing takes place when we forgive, forget, and go on living.

THE MALICE OF SPITE

I believe that some of you reading this book could be healed right now of skin rashes, allergies, heart problems, arthritis, digestive problems, and great inner turmoil if you would forgive that person who has dealt unfairly with you and abandon your plans to "get even!"

Spite will destroy you—I should know. I used to spend my days planning clever phrases to cut people down when they hurt me. I anticipated events even before they occurred. I ground many phantom axes, imagining what I would say if and when the occasion arose.

But when I broke emotionally, spite was one of the first things I had to let go.

Vengeance is a God-sized load. Let Him carry it.

Have you been hurt? If so, what are your plans? Maybe you have been slandered or deceived. Perhaps you have been cheated out of some money, your job, a promotion, a husband, or a wife—what should you do?

We got a call this week from a husband whose wife had just finished destroying every breakable object in their home. We got another call from a woman whose husband is so domineering that she only goes outside the house a few times a year—when he takes her!

The world is filled with builders of prisons and creators of misery. But thank God you do not have to be among them. You may have to live with a person or situation of extremes. But if we approach the situation wisely, most of us could have more liberty than we do.

We often have both men and women tell us how they wish they could attend our Bible study sessions ..., "But my husband (wife) would never agree to it."

In a few cases, that might be true. But more often than not, they are so acclimated to their little prison cells that they would remain inside even if the warden came by and left the door open.

The human mind has great adaptability. Over a period of time, warped can seem straight, sick can appear healthy, and imprisonment can be accepted as final. I meet married couples all the time who are held together by spite. They are literally dedicated to seeking the unhappiness of their partner.

One evening, I was in a card shop looking for a special word to send to someone, when I overheard a man cursing terribly. Curiosity drew me to the other side of the aisle for a look at this person who spewed out the vilest names possible. Do you know what I saw? Standing in the middle of the aisle was an elderly man pushing his crippled wife in a wheelchair. And do you know what he was so angry about? The wife was hesitating about which card to purchase.

The scene was devastating. Here were two persons of advanced years spending their last days on earth impatient, bitter, vile, swearing, and miserable. The woman looked like a confused blank space, and the man had the same snarl I used to see on my father's fox hounds when another dog threatened to interfere with their dinner.

Spite is a deficit in your own personality. You have no reason to continue operating in it, yet there are a million excuses why you should "even the score with life." Prisons are filled with people who chose to go outside the law to balance their ledger. On the other hand, life "on the outside" is filled with people who choose to be criminal to one another in the more acceptable form of emotional assault and battery.

The courts never put us behind bars for destroying the happiness or sanity of another person, but spiteful, vengeful people are nonetheless imprisoned.

Vengeance always has two victims—just as a crime always affects at least two persons: the murderer and the murdered; the robber and the robbed. There is no such thing as a one-victim crime.

The person who sets out in life to even the score is a victim in search of a victim. It may be small, petty emotional crimes against people who love you, or it may be irreversible decisions that bring social or financial collapse to another person.

GETTING EVEN

Marty was a classic case of a spiteful person from the time I first met her. She had been brought up in a reasonably well-balanced household. She was pretty but not the prettiest girl in the family. She was talented, but not the most talented of several siblings. Marty was intelligent but not mentally superior; and, although she was loved, she was not the most loved of all the children.

In the end, Marty developed into a zealous, spiteful adult. Her good nature became bitter and vengeful. She ran with people far below her economic and moral standards and finally married a young man who could never hope to help her gain the status she so desperately sought.

A spiteful person is a wounded person. And he is out to balance the books on wounding. That is, he intends to hurt people just the way he feels he has been wounded.

A spiteful person is a wounded person who feels that life has mistreated him or her. While it may have started out with a circumscribed area, such as family injustice, the person who concentrates on evening the score ultimately blames everybody for his or her misery.

Marty was one of the most generous people I have ever known. She would literally give away her last dollar. On the other hand, if she sensed the least bit of rejection from the person she was helping, she would stab them in the back. Like a dry desert, she could not receive enough applause. If Marty received ten thousand compliments and one negative remark, she only saw the insult. She was the kind of friend with whom you always had to choose your words carefully. While she could take no criticism from anyone else, she was continually pointing out the faults and failures of everyone around her.

Comparison and competition caused her to spend money in excess. It forced her to indulge her children and at the same time demand they excel. It gave her a sharp tongue and a temper subject to fire at any moment. Ultimately, Marty came to believe that any person she could not control disliked her and was her enemy. She finally "paid back" her parents by selling her part of the family estate to a morally seedy family. In her estimation, her spite was justified.

The world for Marty and all spiteful people is divided into two camps—perfect friends and imperfect enemies. These sides are forever changing, depending on the conduct of the people with whom they come in contact.

Spite and revenge are emotional conditions that drain life. But they are also curable. Mental renovation is possible for any person willing to practice the attitude of forgiveness. *Forgiveness* is the key to unlocking the doors for all those prisoners who feel compelled to settle the score with life's offenders.

If you are a person who is continually straightening out the world, either in your mind or with frequent verbal confrontations, then you need to renew your mind concerning spite and revenge. You need to abandon the attitude of having to settle the score with every person who violates your standards.

God says that vengeance is His, and He will repay the offenders. This relieves you and me of the responsibility. In simple language, spite is a waste of good energy. If you have been a victim of score-keeping, let me suggest the following:

1. Every time you are tempted to "get even" with a person, stop! Say "Lord, I commit this situation to You. I forgive that person for what he/she has done, and I ask You to bless him/her."
2. Repeat this every time the situation recurs in your mind.

Given time, your feelings will begin to agree with your new way of thinking. Peace and mental renewal come when our thoughts and attitudes agree with God's way of handling violators. And God's method for any and all offenses is forgiveness.

If you will be free from the emotional drain of spite and revenge, forgive the person and let God settle the account His way.

11

Nature Traps

Human nature is not an easy part of our make-up to describe. Character, attitude, likes and dislikes, temperament, and feelings—all these and more come out of the human constitution. Webster says that human nature is any of the natural instincts, desires, or appetites of man. We might add that it is all man's desires outside of spiritual influence. In other words, human nature begins to exhibit itself from the day we are born. We hardly arrive into the world when we begin to yell and make known our natural desires. Human nature is so aggressive that it considers nothing else but its own desires for the first few years of life.

Think of a child from the day it is born until it is four years of age. Is it common to hear them ask, "Mommy, may I give away and share my toys with other children?" Do many children say, "Mommy, although I do not like green vegetables, because you say I should eat them, I am glad to obey"? Hardly!

The truth is that human nature begins to express itself on day one, and we spend the rest of our lives attempting to bring it under control. If we do not, we should. Everyone who lives with us wishes we would!

Human nature is not an altogether lovely thing. Color preference, taste buds, various spots—these are some of the innocent aspects of our appetites and desires. Cruelty, control, manipulation, perversion, abuse, self-centeredness—these attributes infect the personality and require both personal and social correction.

In this chapter we are going to take a look at human nature and discuss some of the common traps that hang up our lives and emotions. I call them "nature traps." These are the desires and feelings that bring us into bondage instead of the satisfaction we anticipate.

The measuring stick for any action is not the number of immediate benefits it will bring us but what the end result will be. To rob a bank might make us rich for a day, but the end result would be twenty-five years of life behind steel bars.

Human nature operates more by instinct than reason— act, *then* think. We are more inclined to act out of feeling than wait upon reason. But even logic is not the highest thinking. Feelings, desires, and logic all arise from the human nature. They are birthed by instinct and interpreted through past experience. Therefore, any person guided by human nature will find himself continually running into a trap.

Let's be more specific. You are a triad: body, mind, and spirit—this is your present, complete state. From the moment you were born and for all eternity you are spirit. You are an eternal spirit; you live in a body; and you possess a mind.

To acknowledge all three parts of your total self is a great step in the direction of getting your life together. To ignore any one of your three-part composition will sentence you to imbalance as long as you live.

If you were to deny one part of your body, what would happen? Say, for example, you ignored one of your arms—you refused to use it; you refused to clothe it; and you refused to clean it. What would happen to that arm? It would wither and become useless. Not only would your arm become impaired, but your whole body would suffer. Everything you attempted to do would be hindered.

The same is true of anyone who ignores the needs and contributions of one part of their triune make-up. Millions of people are miserable this very moment because they deny the fact that they are spirit beings in need of spiritual direction. Others deny that they have limited bodies and drive themselves into the ground prematurely. Still others ignore the need of their emotional person, and they isolate their minds into a warped lifestyle where they remain miserably alone throughout their lifetime.

God created us a perfect triad. We are well-balanced and productive human beings. The first thing He said to Adam was, "Be fruitful and multiply" (Genesis 1:28). We are designed to reproduce life, balance, order, and happiness among society.

I am not impressed with computers or sophisticated inventions. But I am impressed with the God-designed

machines we call human beings! They invent the wonders. The day a computer invents a person—a living,
loving, compassionate human being, without the help of
man—perhaps I will acknowledge a mechanical marvel.
Until that day, I hold the greatest respect for human beings.

Every person on the face of this earth is a living,
breathing wonder. An eternal spirit, a unique mind, and
a one-of-a-kind body are all wrapped up into one person (repeated four billion times without one duplica-
tion!). What a marvelous creation you are!

Yet, wonderful as we may be intended, most of us
find ourselves walking into various traps throughout our
lifetime. And we find our lot to be filled with more pot-
holes than pleasures.

I have traveled for many years by train, plane, ship,
car, freighter, seaplane, and foot, and I have never yet
met a person who did not have at least one trap in his
or her nature (beginning the list with myself, of course).
Some traps or "bugs" are small and bearable, but some
are so massive they eat up the whole person and everybody who gets caught by them. But small or large, the
traps are there and should be dealt with.

Have you ever heard the saying "That's just my nature"? Perhaps you have excused your conduct with
those very words. I know I have. Actually what we are
attempting to say is, "Yes, that area of my life needs
changing, but I don't intend to make the effort to do so."

Rightly positioned, human nature is a tremendous
possession. Nothing on earth is as powerful as desire.
We feel, desire, act, and possess. What you are is the

choice of your human nature. But the right position of human nature is to acknowledge your triune composition—body, mind, and spirit.

If your *body* rules your life, you will be gluttonous, excessive, and sensual—a lopsided seeker of pleasure.

If your *mind* rules your life, you will be a haughty, selfish, cold, unfulfilled prisoner of pride.

If, on the other hand, you are rightly positioned with the Father of your *spirit*, then you are going to satisfy your body, occupy your mind with healthy thinking and become concerned with eternal pursuits.

NATURE TRAPS OF THE BODY

Let's consider now some of the common bugs found in people who are trapped by the feelings and desires of their body. God identifies these body-traps with the word "carnal:" "To be carnally minded is death..." (Romans 8:6).

If you let the desires of your body rule your life, you will destroy yourself. We have only to look at statistics to see how accurate God's pronouncement is in each generation. "Because the carnal [body bound] mind is enmity against God: for it is not subject to the law of God, neither indeed can be" (Romans 8:7).

Any situation ruled by physical passion is destined to fail. Unless that desire is under the control of the law of life from God, the immature feelings and selfish desires of the five senses will bring death into the best of circumstances. The physical body has no ability to reason. It knows only its own appetite. Like a spoiled child, the body has only one language, and that is desire. It wants what it wants, and it wants it *now!*

What causes smokers to fill their lungs with smoke when conclusive evidence says they are likely to die early with lung disease? The body wants it. What causes a person to continually overeat when statistics say he is cutting years off his life?

A friend of mine went to the doctor with a weight problem. He told her quite frankly that every organ in her body had been displaced. Her three hundred pounds had pushed in on her heart, lungs, liver, and so forth until the doctor concluded that she could not possibly live her normal life span under those conditions.

Do you know what my friend is doing? She is continuing to let her body rule the situation. Huffing and puffing through her young life, disliking herself, embarrassed to be seen by friends her own age, she has yet to tell her body it is no longer running the show.

"Stomach, are you hungry? That's tough!"

"Appetite, do you want junk food? Too bad!"

"Craving, you just have to have a midnight chocolate sundae? Sorry!"

Everywhere I go, I try to help people understand that they can carry on a conversation with their body. The body says, "Desire," and you say, "No!" It is just that simple. "No...no...no...no..!" Even *habits* are broken with this one response.

A few months ago, our son began feeling so tired that he made an appointment with the doctor for a checkup. He slept long hours, dragged through eight hours of work, and came home knocked out and ready for bed.

The doctors examined him only to find a young man in excellent health. "Do you eat well?" Yes. "Smoke?"

No. "Miss sleep?" No. "Take any medication?" No. "How much coffee do you drink in a day"? Twelve cups—sixteen? Or more!

"Try leaving off all caffeine and see what happens."

For one month our son went through a very tough decaffeinating process—no tea, no coffee, and no colas. He had a headache from morning until night. He literally had to make his body drag through work. He felt as though life was hardly worth living. Then light began to spring up. Energy began to return. He slept less but felt more awake.

He no longer had to drink frequent caffeine boosts to keep himself going. He began to operate on real energy, and his body normalized to a sensible level. Now he does not get as high as before, and he also does not fall as low. And occasionally he enjoys a cup—one cup—of coffee.

One of the main themes of God's Word to His people is *moderation*—temperance, the apostle Paul called it. Today's affluent society needs to renew their thinking on self-control more than any other single attitude. *Just because we can afford something does not mean we should have it!*

The body makes a poor leader. This week I sat with a man's man who cried until tears pooled on the floor beside his feet because he had allowed his physical involvement with other women to rob him of the wife of his youth—the woman he still loved after years of separation. "What a fool I was to hurt the person I loved!" he said. "And for what?" He did it for the momentary pleasure of his body.

Bodies have no intelligence. Left to themselves they are purely animal.

One of the greatest social injustices of modern society is to tell people they were born homosexual and that for them it is normal. What hope is there of being liberated from normalcy?

Sexual traps are the product of undisciplined human nature. The result of falling into a sexual trap is a body and mind in control of the spirit.

Any form of immorality is the comic book of great living, an insult to a human being's ability to reason, love, and commit. Immorality produces corny songs, corny movies and television plots, and corny people.

"I just can't control myself" is a five thousand year-old lie. When faced with life and death, most of us find we can do many things we never thought possible. At one point in my life, I wrote my last will and testament because I thought I was going to die. Instead, I found I could do a lot of things I never thought possible.

Within a few months, I made drastic changes in my lifestyle, my way of thinking, and my attitude toward people. I stopped lying to myself; I stopped manipulating other people; I gave up trying to impress the world; and I even stopped flirting with the devil. All my little games went into the garbage can where they belonged, and I got down to the business of real living.

There is no such thing as a body that cannot be disciplined. Once you have your mind made up, simply set down the rules. And don't give an inch—ever!

Yes, your body will cry—so what? It may even have a tantrum. If so, just remind it of the new house rules, and otherwise ignore it.

Is this over-simplification? No more so than our modern exaggeration of the necessity to satisfy every physical urge. Bodies need to be told "no" when they desire unhealthy, excessive, or immoral expressions. A disciplined body is essential to an emotionally healthy life. "For if ye live after the flesh, ye shall die: but if ye through the Spirit do mortify the deeds of the body, ye shall live" (Romans 8:13).

NATURE TRAPS OF THE MIND

Nature traps that arise in the mind manifest another area of our triune composition that calls for discipline. Just as most people are afraid to discipline their bodies, an equal number are also afraid to talk back to their unruly thinking.

- "I have a bad temper; that's my nature."
- "I've tried, but I can't forget when people do me wrong; that's my nature."
- "I cannot tolerate the clumsiness of other people. I am a person who wants it done right, according to my definition."
- "Some people need the crutch of religion. I am sufficient without God."
- "Some people need people; I only need my work—that is my nature."

The babblings of pride are endless. And they will never stop trapping your happiness unless you take definite action against them.

Very few people would allow a nasty relative to move in with them and make havoc of their household. Yet those same people will allow a nasty thought or idea to move into their mental compartment and wreck a good relationship, a good plan, or their peace of mind.

Stop being afraid of your own thoughts. You have authority over them. Say out loud right now:

- "I have authority over my body."
- "My body will do what I say."
- "I will not take orders from the unhealthy desires of my body any longer."

In the same way, I want you to say:

- "I have authority over my mind."
- "My mind will think what I tell it to think."
- "I will no longer tolerate miserable thoughts. But I will throw them out just as I would evict an unwanted house guest."

Now, whenever your body or mind desires wrong things, take effective action. Simply say, "Body (or mind), in the Name of Jesus, I have authority over you, and I say, 'No, you cannot do (or think) that. I bless you with a better plan of action.'"

Simple? Yes. Easy? No. It is the same as retraining a spoiled brat. But it works. And that is, after all, what you are looking for—a solution to your inner turmoil.

THE NATURE OF SPIRIT

Finally, let's take a brief look at your spirit, that part of you capable of living in time and eternity. Bodies wear out and minds grow weary, but the spirit is endless. Your spirit was created to have relationship with God. It is the part of your triune composition capable of the highest type of thinking.

Your spirit is the part of you that aspires to the highest morals, the worthiest goals, and the most honorable relationships. Your spirit, not your mind, is the source of inner harmony and health.

According to recent statistics from the Evangelical World Conference, approximately one-third of the world's people deny the existence of the spirit altogether. Atheists believe their body and mind are the sum total of life.

Another third of the world's people are fanatical religious people who realize the existence of the spirit. They seek to get their life in order by creating spiritual symbols to worship as gods.

The other third of the earth's people acknowledge the existence of the spirit and seek to get themselves rightly related to a living God through the living Person Jesus Christ. It is to these people that I am speaking.

If you believe in God, then you must admit to His description of your make-up. You are an eternal spirit; you live in a body; and you possess a mind.

In First Thessalonians 5:23, Paul said, "I pray God your whole spirit and soul and body be preserved blameless...."

If your life will ever be renewed to a state of peace and inner harmony, then you must learn to rise above the snares and traps of your base human nature. You must learn to live above animal instinct. You must learn to think above mere human logic.

Feelings, desires, and human reason are inadequate guides for the person who chooses to live a life of peace and inner fulfillment along with natural achievement. Only spiritual direction from the living God can adequately empower the human spirit to rise above the clamorings of the mind and body.

Remember, I explained that *the first level of action is instinct or feelings. The second level is reasoning or logic.* But these two levels come out of the human nature—self centered, self-pleasing emotion and passion. The higher and better way of thinking comes when you discipline these two levels and bring them under the authority of *spiritual thinking*—God's way of looking at your life and circumstances.

How can you rid yourself of the traps in your human nature? In the original Greek language, the phrase "cast down" means to destroy violently. When God says to "cast down" reasoning, He means for you and me to take the physical, emotional, and spiritual traps that have been robbing our lives and treat them as we would any life-threatening enemy.

If you developed cancer, what would you do? You would fight it with everything you had. If someone grabbed your child in a store and started running off with him, what would you do? You would pursue that person like a wild animal. This, then, is precisely what you must do to the thieves in your human nature. *Get angry at your weaknesses!* Do not allow them to operate in your life any longer. Despise them. Destroy them. Destroy them. Make them totally unwelcome in your life from this moment forward.

I want you to consider the following three categories of nature traps. This is only a partial list. You may think of others as you examine yourself in the light of the areas I have suggested. As you recognize a familiar snare operating in your life, cast it down and get rid of it. Stop participating in that situation physically, mentally, or spiritually.

BODY TRAPS

The first category we will look at deals with physical habits and compulsions.

Unhealthy Habits
- Smoking
- Drinking
- Excessive eating or not eating enough
- Continual late-night partying
- Nail biting, hair twisting, pulling out eyelashes
- Picking at your skin

Compulsions: *Immorality*
- Adultery (extramarital affairs)
- Fornication (sexual relationships between un-marrieds)
- Homosexuality
- Oral copulation (a compulsion for oral sex rather than genital expression)

- Indecent exposure
- Filthy language
- Pornographic literature or films
- Bestiality (sex with animals)
- Child molesting (any intimate contact with children)
- Compulsive masturbation
- Fantasizing (immoral daydreaming)

Compulsions: *Destructive Actions*
- Physical violence (temper tantrums)
- Withholding affection for extended periods
- A nagging or biting tongue
- Sloppiness and infrequent bathing
- Laziness

Having looked over this suggested list of body traps, did you find some problem areas? If so, I want you to take them one by one and bring them into the light, along with any others you may have written down. You must be completely honest if you want to be completely free.

Now bring them to God, and break your tie with them. Pray out loud: "Father, in the Name of Jesus, I confess that my life is trapped by the sin of _____. I ask You to forgive me. I receive my forgiveness, and I forgive myself."

From this day forward, when any body traps tries to manifest itself in your life, run to God with it. Ask for strength to walk in your liberty and freedom. Resist the destructive desire, and it will eventually lose its hold on you.

MIND TRAPS

Let us look now into the category of mind traps. These are primarily attitudes and thought patterns that you have developed over the years. Remember, you were born with a clear mind. If confusion has been programmed into your thinking, your mind can be re-programmed to produce better results in your emotional life.

Pride:
- Haughtiness
- Concentrating on self
- Feelings of superiority
- Critical attitude
- Gossip and slander
- Perfectionism and intolerance
- Feelings of religious superiority
- Obsession with knowledge
- Control and manipulation of others
- Unforgiveness
- A caustic tongue
- Ingratitude (which produces complaining)
- Boredom

Fears:
- Unknown fears
- Fear of death
- Fear of travel
- Fear of food (anorexia, bulimia)
- Fear of people
- Fear of the dark
- Fear of disease

- Fear of heights and closed places
- Fear of insanity
- Fear of blasphemy

Unstable Thoughts:
- Suspicions—jealousies
- Accusations (against others and self)
- Quitting (in the middle of projects)
- Rejection (of self and others)

Now take the mind traps and do the same thing with them as you did with the physical bondages. Bring them to God and abandon them. Now put a better way of thinking in place of the present traps. "Father God, in the Name of Jesus, I confess to You that I am trapped by thoughts of _____. I ask You to forgive me and set me free from these bondages."

Once you have named them one by one, out loud, I want you to find a verse of Scripture that speaks specifically to your situation—that is, what God thinks about it. Commit God's thoughts to memory. You may need someone to help you locate these Scriptures. Do not be intimidated. Go to church and find someone to help you. Get a concordance. Write these verses down. Put them on your mirror, your refrigerator, or in your billfold, and read them as often as necessary. You will free your mind only as you replace your miserable thoughts with a better way of thinking.

SPIRITUAL TRAPS

The third and final category in nature traps is the area of spiritual snares, in which millions of people find themselves.

Spiritual Fears: Excessive
- Fear of God's punishment
- Fear of blasphemy
- Fear of being unsaved
- Fear of the devil
- Fear of Christians and churches

Spiritual Deceptions: Occult Beliefs
- Denying the existence of Satan
- Cult participation
- Participation in pagan religions
- Idol worship
- Attributing power to man-made objects (jewelry, dolls, etc.)

Spiritual Deceptions: Occult Involvements
- Witchcraft
- Astrology
- Hypnotism
- Seances
- Pagan meditations
- Demonic fashions

Spiritual Delusions:
- A need to be recognized and exalted
- An unrealistic image of your spiritual powers
- Feelings of being spiritually "special"
- A need for spiritual control over people
- A belief that you are one of the great ancient prophets.

- Believing that God has called you to abandon your family for a ministry
- Being excessively demon-conscious

The cure for problems in this category is not a one time confession. You need to be taught correctly over a period of time. If you have trouble with one or more areas of spiritual bondage, then you need to make a list. Take this list to a known, respected, balanced, and spiritually alive pastor. Choose a minister who is knowledgeable in the Word of God and familiar with the work of the Holy Spirit. Be open about your fears and involvements. God can bring your spiritual life back into sensible balance. Thousands of people are finding complete spiritual restoration.

In the meantime, know this:

- If you are worried about whether you have blasphemed against God, then you have not. *Blasphemous people are not concerned about spiritual matters.*
- If you have repented of your sins, committed your life to Jesus, confessed your faith in Him, and been baptized, then you are saved. Never mind those doubtful feelings. The fact is what the Word says: "Whosoever shall call on the name of the Lord shall be saved" (Acts 2:21).
- If you have been involved in the occult, all you need to do is renounce it, abandon any contact with it, and forget about it.
- If you have been deluded by personal thoughts of spiritual grandeur, then close the door on them.

No one person is more special to God than the other. God loves us all equally. Whatever He will do for one, He will do for all who come to Him in sincerity.

12

Nature's Tranquilizers: Tears, Laughter, and Music

A few years ago, Paul and I were ministering at a men's retreat. A young man about twenty-five or so came up to me during lunch and said, "This has been one of the greatest days I've had since I was a young boy. You see, I got into drugs several years ago—then alcohol, the sex scene, and all that goes with it. I became so embittered that I turned to ice inside. This morning, during the meeting, I cried for the first time in years. I didn't think it was possible for me to feel again."

What a beautiful and painless way to get mentally renovated—he experienced a washing away of years of crust with one good cry.

"Put off...the old man, which is corrupt according to the deceitful lusts; And be renewed in the spirit of your mind" (Ephesians 4:22-23).

That young man had been deceived by chemical highs, liquid depressants, and physical fantasies. He had been on a childish merry-go-round for so many years that his real emotions had been paved over. One good cry did not solve all his problems, of course, but it did open a flood of pent-up feelings that cleared the path to mental renovation.

Another time, in a prison visiting room, I sat opposite a strong ex-policeman whose eyes kept filling with tears. Finally, I reached over and put my hand on him. "You know, I think you need to have a good cry," I encouraged. He complied with a good minute of fluid tranquillity, after which we went on with a pleasant conversation.

I believe our twentieth-century pseudo-sophistication is robbing us of a great emotional release that comes through tears and laughter. God says, "They that sow in tears shall reap in joy (singing)" (Psalm 126:5). Spiritual tears, compassionate tears, tears of repentance, and tears of gratitude wash the soul clean and set the heart to singing.

Yes, I know we are told not to get over-emotional about religious matters, but Dr. Luke (7:38) records the story of a woman who once came to Jesus. She knelt down in front of everyone present, washed Jesus' feet with her *tears*, and wiped the tears away with the hair on her head. Now that is emotion, is it not?

Probably few churches would permit such an act today. Yet, Jesus did not stop the woman. He did not say, "Mary, stop crying! You are just getting carried away." No, Jesus said of the weeping woman, "Her sins, which are many, are forgiven; for she loved much" (Luke 7:47).

The apostle Paul was an educated, aggressive man who considered it beneficial to cry, saying of his work,

"I ceased not to warn every one night and day with tears" (Acts 20:31).

Jeremiah, the rugged, uncompromising prophet of Israel who was rejected by his own family, his home town, the religious hierarchy, and the government, said he wished his eyes were a "fountain of tears" (Jeremiah 9:1).

Rejection and frustration are like a coral reef. Unless we find a release valve for them, they will build an impenetrable wall of internal hardness around our lives. But tears are one of nature's available resources to prevent this emotional isolation.

Do you know what resulted from Jeremiah's weeping over the Jews while they were exiled in Babylon? Upon hearing the Word of God, the people began to take stock of themselves. They cried so loudly you could not distinguish the tears from the laughter.

If you are in captivity, cry!

If you have been set free, cry!

Men, it will soften your heart to cry. Women, it will relieve the tensions you have built up in the course of the day. Young people, it is *cool* to cry. Tears are a spiritbirthed release from life's pressures. God created you with this safety valve. Use it instead of taking unhealthy chemicals.

If you would rather repress your emotions and get heart trouble, go ahead.

If you husbands and wives are so "adult" that you cannot cry together, then let your marriage crust over and petrify. Paul and I have a ball crying over touching scenes, stories, and special times with the Lord—and whatever else touches us together.

God created human beings with emotions as surely as He gave us intellect. He tells us through wise King Solomon "There is a time to weep..." (Ecclesiastes 3:4). It is not all the time, but it is some of the time.

Excessive control of your emotions is as unhealthy as excessive release. There is an appropriate time for tears. But they must be genuine tears if they are to bring genuine release to you. Phony liquid, attention-getting outbursts, morbid self-pity, wailing, and wallowing do nothing for the actor but give him a cheap moment on the stage. But real tears, springing out of real feelings, are clean, refreshing fountains of release.

Hezekiah was a king when he learned he was going to die. Despite his royal position, he cried. God saw his tears and gave him fifteen more years of life. Many of us would lengthen our lives today if we would abandon our stuffy little images and have ourselves a good cry.

If your emotions have you tied up over a situation and you have the urge to cry, liquefy the feelings and release a new way of thinking on the subject.

You are a person with an endless supply of emotional wealth. You are a valuable coin with tears on one side and that marvelous rejuvenator called laughter on the other.

LAUGHTER

Ecclesiastes 3:4 tells us there is "a time to weep, and a time to laugh."

I love to laugh. Like the song from Mary Poppins says, "I love to laugh, loud and long and clear, I love to laugh; it's getting worse every year!"

I thank the Lord that I come from a family who loves to laugh. Every special gathering has always been generously seasoned with joking, hugging, talking, and laughing. Good, clean laughter is a favorite guest at our house.

Recently one of my brothers came for a visit. "Sit down and listen to this," he said smiling. We had no idea what to expect as he placed a recording on the stereo and turned it on. We heard a single laugh, then two laughs, and then three—all of us began to crack up and then had a good two-minute, emotional renewal. It was a recording of nothing but laughter.

"A merry heart doeth good like a medicine" (Proverbs 17:22).

"A merry heart maketh a cheerful countenance" (Proverbs 15:13).

People who can laugh not only look better but, in fact, apply medicine to their emotions. Gripe all the way to the drug store, or laugh and spend your money at the ice cream parlor.

A few years ago, we decided to have a yard sale. As Paul's nature goes, he was making the best of an otherwise humdrum morning. Like an auctioneer, he was entertaining everybody with grand explanations of the treasures spread out before them.

A little sawed-off truck of sorts came wheeling in, and two elderly men got out to join our camaraderie.

"Well, here come two fine gentlemen in search of a rare purchase. What can I do for you fine men today?" Paul said enthusiastically.

"What is this?" those crusty old seniors snarled. "I'm not buying anything from you!" And with that, they fumed their way back across the street, got into their pickup, and roared away.

What those two men needed was a complete overhaul of their sense of humor. A little humor injected into a trying situation can make it completely bearable.

We twentieth-century people take ourselves too seriously. Today's home is so adult that it is boring. Small children are consulted as though the responsibility of the home were theirs. They are pushed to achieve and behave as adults. They are corrected and belittled for crying or laughing in the wrong places.

I watched Dr. Grace Mitchell, psychologist and educator, being interviewed. Do you know what she said she would like to see written across the wall of every day-care center in this country? "Joy."

Years ago I used to listen to psychologist Dr. Clyde Narramore on the radio. Even then he was trying to warn parents that children should be allowed to be children. At a time when children should be out and close to nature, laughing and playing with their friends, they are in the house doing homework—even in grammar school—pushing for college. But what about pushing for happiness and sound emotions?

Has your home lost its tolerance for tears and laughter? Is good, clean jesting a part of your family's emotional expression? How often does your family laugh together?

What about you personally? Would people say that you have a good sense of humor? Can you laugh at yourself? If you make a blunder, can you laugh about it, or are you touchy and sensitive?

Pent-up emotion is dangerous. It is unhealthy for your body; it is unhealthy for your mind; and it is unhealthy for society.

Nations, just like individuals, need a sense of humor. As I travel around the world, I see whole nations of wound-up or beaten-down people—people who have forgotten how to smile, laugh, and roll with the punches.

One day Paul and I left for the shopping center. At a traffic light, one car violated the rights of another in some small way. The offended driver jumped out of his car, ran up to the other driver, punched him in the face, knocked him down on the pavement, split open his head, ran to his car, and took off. In a matter of two minutes, before anyone could stop him, he inflicted great harm on a perfect stranger.

God has given human beings two simple, harmless, and fun ways to release emotions and feelings. Tears and laughter are relaxing, natural refreshments that allow people to live together with a minimum of friction.

I think it is time we take off our sophisticated, legalistic faces and forget our programmed responses. We need to renew our sense of humor and begin to be real people with each other. We can become real people once again if we will renew our sense of humor.

In Romans 12:15, God tells us how to begin this process of renewing our ability to laugh and cry: "Rejoice with them that do rejoice, and weep with them that weep."

In other words, take your eyes off yourself. Take an interest in people around you. If someone tells you something sad and you want to cry, then cry. Water that lump in your throat with good, warm tears.

If someone is telling you something humorous and you want to laugh, forget about that yellow degree hanging on your wall, unbutton your coat, lean back, and have a good round of jolly ha! ha! ha! Remember, if Christians forget how to weep and laugh at the right things, the devil will teach the world how to weep and laugh at the morbid, the pornographic, and the sacrilegious. Modern movies, books, and television themes are perfect examples of this. Sick humor flourishes where a lack of healthy humor exists.

People are created with an emotional need to express themselves through reasonable tears and laughter. The day I looked into the mirror and could not smile, I knew I was in trouble. I had no tears or laughter to release my misery. It took a few months of reprogramming my mind with the joy-filled words of God, but I stuck to the task until I was thoroughly renovated.

If you have lost your sense of humor—if you can no longer feel with other people's fortunes and misfortunes or can no longer identify with your own healthy emotions—then may I suggest a sure cure for your renewal? It will not restore you overnight, but if it is taken regularly, you will be the happy person you once were.

1. Fill your mind with the thoughts of God. Read and think (meditate) on the truths stated in the Bible. Take one thought and go over and over it until it is clearly imprinted in your mind.

2. The second spiritual prescription I recommend for all emotional problems is God's wonder drug called *singing*.

THE TOUCH OF MELODY

In the same letter where Paul says we can be renewed in the spirit of our minds, he also says, "Speaking to yourselves in psalms and hymns and spiritual songs, singing and making melody in your hearts to the Lord; Giving thanks always for all things unto God...in the name of our Lord Jesus Christ" (Ephesians 5:19-20).

This is the eternal wonder-drug for renewing your burned-out, dried-up minds, hearts, and emotions. Sing songs of praise and thanksgiving to God. Nothing will revive you like spiritual singing.

I simply cannot say enough about music. Yes, *listen* to spiritual music, but *sing!* You need to sing out loud every day, throughout the day, as long as you live. Spiritual music is healing.

We have had countless people tell us they were at the breaking point when they began listening to music of joy, worship, and praise; and they were emotionally turned around.

Tears, laughter, and music—what a prescription for mental health! And the only cost to you is effort—discipline and effort.

Speak to your mind. The apostle Paul said it two thousand years ago by inspiration of God. I say it today from personal experience. Do not be afraid to speak to your emotions. Reprogram your mind with happy thoughts. Sing out loud at the top of your voice. Sing songs of praise and rejoicing.

If you want to be restored emotionally, cry, laugh, and sing.

Do you remember that I said we are a family with a great sense of humor? We are also people who know how to share our tears, and we are always and forever singing.

The English tradition of singing has been a part of our family since we were old enough to carry a tune. I never let a day go by that I do not continue that natural and spiritual heritage.

My father was a man's man—tough, aggressive, and an expert marksman. He frequently filled our home with his rich, bass voice. Mother had no vibrato, but she also pierced the walls with her old Methodist hymns. We children were and are rich with music in our own lives.

Cry if you have to; laugh if you want to; and sing because you need to! Nature's tranquilizers are with you wherever you go. Take them as often as needed.

13

Marital Refreshment

Since I am addressing a number of emotional problems common to all people, I cannot adequately cover the giant of marital conflict. However, I do want to address a basic, simple solution that will bring a breath of fresh air into the humdrum situation many people find themselves in by virtue of having said, "I do."

The subject is *physical appearance*. We human beings often overlook the obvious in our mad search for the complex. Life—and therefore marriage—is as simple as the amount of common sense we possess about it. You do not need a Ph.D. to develop the fine art of living. Your God-given common sense is one of the greatest gifts you possess and is invaluable to eliminating the frustrations of living.

Something as simple as physical appearance may seem relatively unimportant in the great emotional struggles we face daily. "Combing my hair cannot possibly help the brain that sits underneath it."

Not so! Out of my own experiences with emotional upheaval, I have learned that the first thing I can do to start my day right is to get up, look at myself in the mirror, and make every improvement possible. It is important to bathe, dress, and physically prepare yourself for interaction with people.

Physical appearance is the first thing emotionally disturbed people let go. You will never go into a mental hospital and find everyone well-groomed.

A friend of mine has periodic manic-depressive months when she is almost out of touch with reality. During these periods, she always allows her hair to become oily and stringy. She wears the same dress for weeks, applies no make-up, and takes no baths unless she is forced.

When I went to visit her recently, I knew there had been a drastic improvement the minute I walked in. How? She was sitting up and smiling with a fresh hairstyle, clean clothes, and pink cheeks.

Good grooming lifts your own attitude about yourself as well as the attitude of those people who live with you. No, it is not a cure-all. Even well-groomed people have problems. But physical appearance does affect the freshness and interest ratio of a person, especially in the marriage relationship.

In this chapter, we are going to take a look into that "mirror, mirror on the wall."

Do you recall the classic story of the queen who owned a talking mirror? Well, many of us get a talking mirror after we are married; but unlike the queen's mirror, our mirror lies to us.

INVESTMENT BENEFITS

As I have stated throughout this book, honesty is the road to recovery. Being honest with yourself is essential if you will ever develop emotional and mental stability.

Let me ask you a question: How much time do you invest in your marriage? Please do not say all of your time, because if you were not married you would still have a lot of the same daily responsibilities you perform right now. What I want you to answer for yourself honestly is, "How much time do you invest in your appearance?"

When Adam saw Eve, he was not looking for a zoo keeper, a financial analyst, a fruit inspector, or even a drill sergeant. Natural Adam was lonely. God saw Adam's plight and said, "It is not good that the man should be alone." (Genesis 2:18).

Humanly speaking, I believe we are all Adam. And I do not believe that Eve was standing there in bubble curlers and a faded bathrobe the first time Adam laid eyes on her. I also think Adam jumped up and ran to the nearest drug store for a package of razor blades and a bottle of Listerine.

How do you rate your daily appearance—excellent, good, or poor? How do you rate your appearance in comparison to the days when you were trying to "trap" your partner? Is your appearance the same, better, or worse?

Are you as well-groomed as the women who work with your husband (or the men who work with your wife)?

How many pounds does your partner wish you would accidentally misplace—*permanently?* I am not talking about diet-mania bordering on starvation, just a size agreeable to you both. Or how many pounds does your partner wish you would *find* so you would have the energy to do something besides drive yourself to the doctor with a hunger headache?

Does your husband think your hair has turned into three-inch rolls of pink foam? Does your wife think you have contracted a "weekend allergy" to combs, razor blades, and showers?

If you think physical appearance is not important, I want you to read these words from Exodus 19:10-11: "And the Lord said unto Moses, Go unto the people, and sanctify them today and tomorrow, and let them wash their clothes...for the third day the Lord will come down in the sight of all the people...."

In the Old Testament, the priests had to be spotlessly clean in body and clothing before they ministered.

One of the greatest acts ever performed for Jesus— in *His* opinion—was when a woman washed His feet and poured costly perfume on them.

In Proverbs 31:22, God describes a virtuous woman's appearance. "She maketh herself coverings of tapestry; her clothing is silk and purple." Now that is a far cry from dingo boots and a sweatshirt!

In fact, Proverbs 31 says that a *wise woman's* husband will go to work and brag about her. And of course, the husband will surely dress in such a way that the people at work won't say, "If your wife looks so nice, then why is she married to you?"

I am not talking about "Virginia Trim" and "Ronald Rich." I am talking about using common sense and prayer for guidance to keep yourself looking attractive to your partner in the most valuable human relationship you have on earth. If you are on a desperate budget, then do what Paul and I do—go to a good outlet shop, and buy the final sale. The "final sale" means they'll practically pay you to take the clothes off the rack for them! We do this because, as married people, we have a responsibility to keep ourselves looking nice in the eyes of our husband or wife. We owe each other that pleasure.

ATTITUDE ADJUSTMENT

It is one thing to "look nice," but it is another to *be* nice. I do not care if you look like you stepped off the cover of a fashion magazine—I do not care if you, *in fact*, stepped off the cover of a fashion magazine—or if you are the head of General Motors, a doctor, lawyer, merchant, or chief. If you are a pain to live with, then you are a pain! Just as many tears fall onto plush carpet as fall onto bare floors.

I often hear people say, "I'd rather be rich and miserable than poor and miserable." Well, I'd rather not be miserable, period!

One evening, my husband and I were having dinner at a restaurant with a young couple, and it appeared that the waiter had forgotten to bring the husband's dessert. We were all finished, and he was still waiting. Finally, his wife spoke up. "Honey, I think you will have to skip your dessert or we will be late for the concert."

When she said that, I observed the reaction of that well-educated, supposedly mature man. He pursed out his lips like a three-year-old, folded his arms in defiance, and was about to rebut when he spied his dessert coming. All of a sudden it was as though the street bully had just decided to return his little red wagon. What congeniality he displayed!

Married people have disagreements. A minor explosion now and then will not hurt anything if you keep it minor and let it die quickly. But constantly stamping your feet, demanding your way, blowing off steam in public, ruining family holidays with temper tantrums, carrying your feelings on your shoulder, and refusing to talk makes life miserable.

Jesus said, "Blessed are the peacemakers" (Matthew 5:9). I might add, cursed are the peace breakers!

Christians can be just as childish and spoiled—just as joy-killing—as anybody else. This is a shame because we have the Spirit of God to help us control our emotions.

In fact, I know I would be considerably more selfish and demanding if God did not side with Paul part of the time. He will, you know. God will take your partner's side when you are out of order. And if He has never corrected you, then either you are terribly good or else you are not listening well.

God cares how we treat each other, and that includes your partner. Many times I want to stay angry and enjoy the misery just a little longer, but I made a decision several years ago never to waste another day of my life on something foolish.

We who are married know that nothing goes right when things at home go wrong. Marital misery is twenty-four hours a day, and it accompanies you everywhere you go. Consequently, when I decided never to *waste another day of my life*, that meant I could not go around sulking or griping all day long at my husband. Never mind who is at fault. Just ask yourself, "Is this disagreement worth one whole day of my life? Is it really that important?" If the answer is "no," then force yourself to change the subject and your tone of voice. You may not *feel* like it, but feelings will follow soon after you change the subject.

How sad it is to know couples who have devoted their entire lives to making each other miserable or to be among couples who switch partners like flavors of ice cream, hoping for a perfect person. Life is too short and marriage can be too wonderful to waste it on a sloppy appearance, temper tantrums, or unrealistic expectations. With effort, you can court your partner every day of your brief life together and make your journey extremely rewarding.

If you would decide to renew your relationship with the person you fell in love with, all kinds of possibilities would begin to surface in your mind.

A young man recently made a statement about his wife that Paul often declares about me: "I don't know what I would do without her." What a beautiful tribute! I feel the same way about Paul. We are not only husband and wife but best friends, pals, and buddies—fully committed to each other's welfare.

Do we ever disagree, argue, or get disgusted? Of course! We are natural, and human nature, undisciplined, is self-centered. But we never hold on to the ill-will created by our differences. Our disagreements always suffer a short life span. We both see to that.

I would not dream of devoting an entire day to grinding over some fault or mistake of my husband's. That would mean I would have to go a full day without talking to God! Oh, yes, you cannot be angry, resentful, and unforgiving toward a person and enjoy spiritual fellowship with the God of love and forgiveness. It simply will not work.

Paul and I got into an argument driving down the streets of Atlanta, Georgia one day. When we arrived at our destination, Paul got out and slammed the door. I was left steaming.

"Lord, I think I won't speak to him for the next three days," I said.

"Then don't bother talking to me either," came a quick, inward reply!

Husbands and wives, if you are having major problems and need an impartial referee, go to your minister and do what he advises. If your marriage has lost its shine, then get busy. Start with that physical house you call your body, and bring it into shape. Buy some cologne, and spray it on a new dress or shirt. Encourage your tired face with a little help, and put a few curls in your hair first thing in the morning. If you do not see each other all day, then prepare for an early evening appointment that is more important to your happiness than any person you will meet all day.

You only have one natural life to live. Each day has twenty-four wonderful hours in it. If you have a husband or wife, you are doubly blessed because you have someone with whom to share your life. Neither you nor your partner is perfect. Perhaps you cannot share everything you wish with them, but at least you are not alone. And whether or not they applaud, every man and woman appreciates a clean, fresh physical appearance coupled with a good disposition.

Why don't you thank God right now for your partner? Ask Him to show you how to be the kind of person that will bring joy and fulfillment into the marriage relationship.

14

Love

Human beings have three basic *physical needs:* food, clothing, and shelter. You could not live without any one of these physical provisions. Human beings have two basic *spiritual needs:* to repent and to worship. Every one of us wants to be free of guilt. And we have such a hunger to worship that if we cannot find the true God, we will create one of our own out of wood, bronze, jade, or money.

Human beings have two basic *emotional needs:* to love and to be loved. No person will ever be emotionally overcome if they have a healthy flow of love that is giving as well as receiving.

This flow of love is what we are going to talk about in this chapter.

Have you ever stopped to think about what brought you into this world? The answer is *love.* Love is what brought you into existence. Quite possibly the love of

171

two persons—your mother and father—and the expression of their love for each other brought your natural body into existence. If you had the ideal situation, home was the natural residence of love where you were nurtured and cared for. With the example of caring parents and relatives, you should have grown quite naturally into a loving person who can both give and receive affection.

This is the kind of home I knew all the days of my childhood. What fortunate people we are to be allowed to develop in an atmosphere of love.

While our home was not perfect, it was warm and filled with loving compassion for each other. Hateful words and acts simply were not tolerated. Nothing that injured love was acceptable to my parents. Name-calling, swearing, lying, stealing, fighting—any one of these acts prompted strong discipline from our five-foot mother who had a switching-arm like a gladiator! And we still love her today for such careful and exhaustive training.

My sister, Dr. Sharon Wooten, Ph.D. in curriculum development, says, "Nothing is better for children than love and discipline. It is imperative to good education. It works for young people everywhere."

Love and discipline are ideal principles that work well in every area of life. Yet many of you were not born into the ideal situation or raised with loving discipline. You may have been loved, or you may have been unwanted and rejected. But regardless of how you came into this world, the moment you received the spark of life, God breathed an eternal plan into your soul. It is a plan that is to last a lifetime.

Above and beyond all physical circumstances, the love of God brought you into existence. You will never be too young or grow too old for the love and purpose of God. His plan is ideal for you.

We are told in Paul's letter to the church at Colosse to "Put on charity [love] which is the bond of perfectness" (Colossians 3:14).

The word *bond* means "joint tie, uniting principle." It is like the ligaments that hold your bones together. You might compare it to glue. Love is the *glue* that holds life together.

In that same Pauline sentence, the word *perfectness* means "complete"—complete in growth, labor, mental character, and moral character.

In other words, this is what God says to you and me about the number one emotional need of mankind: "Put love into your mind and emotions. It is the glue that holds your life together! Your *maturity*, your *work*, your *mind*, and what you are *morally*, are all knit together by love."

You need to *receive* love if you want to be whole and harmonize body, mind, and spirit. You need to give love to other people if you want to keep the flow of wholeness working for your mental well being and the health of society.

I overheard my husband Paul talking with a woman on the phone one day. During the conversation, he kept trying to dig through the rubble of her emotional collapse. When he hung up the phone, his comment was, "That woman is simply starved to death for love. She will never be healed unless someone comes along who will give love to her."

173

Mental and emotional health are not possible outside love. When you were conceived, you were surrounded and protected by your mother's womb. Never mind the conditions of the world around you—you were safe and protected by the womb. *Love* is exactly like a womb for you and me once we are birthed into this world. We cannot survive the diseases of life without the protection of love.

At this moment, you may be saying to yourself, "It all sounds good, but I don't have any love to give, and I don't have anybody to give me love." If so, then I want to share a beautiful truth with you. There is Someone who loves you with an eternal affection. You have an endless supply if you will only take advantage of it: *God is love!* Divine love is as endless as God himself. There is no need ever to run out of love.

How much love does God have for you?

"Many, O Lord my God, are thy wonderful works which thou hast done, and thy thoughts which are to us-ward: they cannot be reckoned up in order unto thee: if I would declare and speak of them, they are more than can be numbered" (Psalm 40:5).

God loves you so much that He *thinks* about you more times than a modern calculator could enumerate. "More than can be numbered." Too often we meet people who declare that God has nothing to do with their life. They manage quite well without Him. Baloney! This entire earth is wrapped in the womb of the divine love and favor of God. The day it is not, this world will fall apart just as surely as unloved people become unglued once they are denied reasonable affection.

Remember, you are held together by love. As long as you live on this earth, the love of God will be with you, reaching out to and calling you into relationship with Him. Many people are miserable, frustrated, lonely, afraid, sick, and in trouble because they are running from love. They run from the love of God, and they run from the love of people.

Most of us can "give" much more easily than we can "receive." To receive love from another human being is difficult. Love obligates us to open up, respond, and admit to our need.

Love exposes the real us. It shows what we are made of. And most of us do not want to admit that we are held together with something so *tender* as love. We would rather be held together by macho power, forces, aggressive liberation, intellect, Elmer's glue—anything but love: patient, generous, courteous, kind, humble, compassionate, enduring, self-controlled, even-tempered, trusting, righteous, forgiving, faithful, positive, and never failing love!

I just gave you God's definition of love from chapter thirteen of First Corinthians.

This is the bond, the glue, that holds you together and causes you to be truly successful in life. This is the good news—the affectionate Gospel—that God wants to share with you and the world.

- When you are *impatient,* you break down the bond of love that holds you together. It may be a small or a large impatience. But if you practice impatience, you injure your own sound, God-designed make-up...because love is *patient*.

- If you are *hate-filled*, you destroy the seams of kindness that unite your life with others...because love is *kind*.

- If you are *greedy and stingy*, generosity is wiped out of your life, along with its fulfilling benefits...because love is *generous*.

- If you are *discourteous*, you will get hateful remarks made back to you by others...because love is *courteous*.

- If you are *uncaring*, you will attract cold, impersonal responses from others...because love *cares*.

- If you are *arrogant*, then not even your friends will like you, and you will be lonely...because love is *humble*.

- If you *give up easily*, you will always attract failure...because love *endures*.

- If you lack *self-control*, you will have a miserable home as well as wretched working conditions...because love is *self-control*.

- If you are *cruel, irritable, and volatile*, you will never be sure of a good day because your temper will keep robbing you of joy...because love is *even-tempered*.

- If you are *suspicious* of everything and everybody you meet, you will miss all of life's good surprises—good friends, good business deals, and good opportunities—because love is *trusting*.

- If you are *unrighteous,* then you will miss all the joys of knowing God and will never know the treasures God has for you in the Spirit. You will miss the eternal things in life...because love is *righteous.*
- If you are *unforgiving,* you will be bound by your own sins all your life. Jesus said that if you forgive, you will be forgiven...because love is *forgiving.* (See Mark 11:25.)
- If you are *unfaithful and undependable,* you will miss the reward of every good venture you begin. You will always stop short of success...because love is *faithful.*
- If you are *negative,* you will repel love all your life from every person who offers it...because love is *positive.*

Love never fails, and you will never fail with divine love.

GOD LOVES YOU

Do you see that love is the necessary ingredient for successful living? With love, your home, your work, and your personal life can and will hold together.

Perhaps you do not have any natural love to share with another person. You may see yourself as someone without any feelings of love. If you are emotionally wounded, you no doubt feel drained of all feeling. This is the number one statement I receive from people who are suffering mentally or emotionally: "I don't feel anything."

"Never mind your feelings," I always respond. "They are dishonest. Because you are wounded emotionally, your feelings will give you false readings. Like a damaged appliance, your feelings are untrustworthy. You *do* have to give, and you do have a capacity to receive love. The capacity for love is divinely created, and you will *never* be without it."

Do you *know* God loves you just the way you are? He loves you even when you are broken, wrecked, unfinished, in bits and pieces, fearful, and failing. He loves you!

God will not leave you as you are, hurting and incomplete. When His love has its perfect way, God will change you around so much that you will end up looking and feeling whole, sound, sane, complete, and even perfect.

When God's love heals a wounded person, he goes right out and falls in love with people—and people fall in love with him.

You were brought into this world with the very hairs of your head numbered. You were designed on a special drawing board. Your home, your city, your country, and your nationality were carefully selected for you. Jesus even said your height was predetermined.

Take a good look at yourself right now. The same God who created the world designed you. He likes the way you look on the outside, and He likes the way you look on the inside. The interior part of you, your spirit, is in fact God's residence.

After God finished designing you, He said, "Here is another temple." You are a living, breathing, and holy residence for the Creator of the universe. That makes you very important. Just as your home is the most important place on earth to you, God's "temples" are of the utmost concern to Him. He could have spun a star-studded castle just above the earth for His residence, but He chose instead to live within you and me. I personally feel honored by His choice of a home place, don't you?

In addition to choosing to live within your life, God sent His Son to teach you the way to live in optimum health and happiness. He paid the price for your repeated violations. Therefore, when you come to Him with a handful of liabilities, He can say, "I forgive them."

You may have stepped down from the control center of your life and received Jesus as Lord. If so, He has given you His Name to use, coupled with all the legal rights of the supernatural authority of heaven. You have His Word, which will stand by you continually and make sense out of your confusion. Jesus guarantees you eternal life when you leave this natural world, thus removing the dread of death. In other words, we can surely agree with King David when he declares that God "daily loadeth us with benefits" (Psalm 68:19).

You are loved. Whether or not you *feel* it at the moment, you *are* greatly loved. And you will be loved throughout eternity, if you want to be. All that is required of you is to reach out to the God who is love. All other gods have rules. Material gods have power. But only the true and living God has love.

You are loved by the living God. As long as you live on this earth you will be loved by God every day of your life. You can never sink too low or climb too high that

His love cannot reach you. But you will only receive the full benefits of His love if you receive His Son Jesus. Jesus is the umbilical cord connecting you to the womb of divine love and feeding your mind the nutrition it needs in order to be healthy.

Ask any doctor, and he will verify that sick emotions will eventually produce sick bodies. Love, on the other hand, can and does restore health. Many bodies, drained of life because no one cares, can be restored. Love-starved people become emotionally unbalanced. Loneliness is an unnatural state. It is equivalent to ripping a baby from its mother's womb and throwing it to the ground. Without love we either starve or become terribly malnourished.

Starve a person of love, and he or she will become emotionally or mentally unstable. Emotional and mental problems create physical stress. Physical stress with no letup wears down the body, allowing disorder and disease to strike.

During her lifetime, Corrie ten Boom told many stories of the stark contrasts between hate and love. Imprisoned in a concentration camp during World War II, Corrie learned the power of God's love to nourish and strengthen the body and the emotions. One such story that stands out in my mind concerns a night when she felt especially afraid and alone. Her mind wandered back to a more comfortable scene from her childhood when her father, tucking her into bed at night, would place his big hand lovingly on her face. She cried that night in that barren prison, "Heavenly Father, would you put your big hand on my little face tonight?"

Dependable, unfailing, unconditional love is the anchor for human mental stability. There simply is no substitute. The only question remaining is, "How can we receive such love?"

The answer is obvious: by receiving the love of God through His Son, Jesus. This is the way to receive love that never fails us!

LOVING OTHERS

Remember, I stated at the beginning of this chapter that human beings have two basic emotional needs: to love and to be loved. You can be loved by God fully and richly through His Son Jesus. But you also have an equal need to return His love to Him.

How can you return the love of God to Him and keep that healing, stabilizing power flowing in your life? How can you develop that love relationship between you and Him that feeds your life with fulfilling happiness?

The answer is *twofold*. First, God is a person and must be approached, conversed with, respected, honored, and pursued the way you reach out to any potential lover. The line of communication must be kept open daily between you and God. We call this *worship*.

In addition to our worship of God, we must also *love people* if we are going to love Him back in a fully satisfying manner. People are God's property, concern, and creation. God cares about people! To worship is one side of the picture, and to love people is the other side. I live my life continually looking for an opportunity to give some person something I think will make him happy.

We once stayed in the home of a young mother whose responsibility to cook for us kept her in the kitchen several hours a day. At the end of our visit, I had a desire to do something special for her great efforts. As soon as I returned home, I went straight to my "special" store and had a ball selecting several things I envisioned just for her. Here is a portion from her letter of response:

Dear Mona:

> WHAT A SURPRISE! What a surprise it was to receive that big package. It was just like Christmas when I opened it, and I was just as excited. And the more we pulled out, the more there was. We could not believe our eyes. We expected *a* blouse or *a* skirt. Everything fit to a tee! The blouse is beautiful and makes me feel very special. I felt so guilty and thought, "I wish I could bless her in such a way!" All I can say is, "The Lord richly bless you *abundantly!*"

AGAPE LOVE

How can you and I love people? By helping them and meeting their needs. By reaching out and helping some other person find their happiness, we put love into action. This is happiness on its way to full explosion in your life. When I look around at this great world of opportunity, I do not believe any person would be bored or unhappy if they were busy loving people.

Love does not have to be accompanied by emotion. You do not have to "feel" anything to love people, although "feelings" are certain to be birthed sooner or later. But pure love is not based on feeling.

Pure love is not emotional excitement. It is not physical chemistry or sloppy permissiveness. *Genuine love is divine opportunity to bless, to forgive, to help, to accommodate, to encourage, and to inspire one another as we go about the process of living.*

Many marriages could be saved; many relationships could be restored; and many children could be salvaged if only we understood the principle of real love. Certainly many people could be restored emotionally if we got down to the business of loving.

If you want to receive love, receive Jesus. If you want to give love, worship God; then go out and take every opportunity you can find to bless people. Jesus said the entire sum of the Scriptures is to love God with all your heart and to love your neighbor as yourself. (See Matthew 22:37-40.)

There was a time in my life when circumstances were so unbearable I almost completely lost my emotional and physical health. As far as I could see, I was hopelessly trapped in a room with no doors or windows. This situation lasted ten long years of my life. But in spite of the misery, they were years of profit. I was held together with the bonds of love I bridged between myself and other people. I literally *gave* my way into sanity. I gave of myself, my time, my home, and every material object I could possibly spare. I literally survived on the joy of realizing I had made someone else happy.

Are you depressed? Anxious? Afraid? Lonely? Confused? Bored? Then go out, find a need, and meet it! Your life will be held together through *loving renewal.*

I am going to ask you to do something that you may have never done before. I am going to ask you to say out loud the word "love."

Now please say, "I am loved," and "I am filled with the love of God...therefore I can love." Having said that, now say, "I love You, Father God. I love You, Lord Jesus. I love You, Holy Spirit."

Finally, will you take one more step? Will you tell someone you know that you love them? If you can't say it, write it.

It may take everything you have inside and out to do it, but go ahead! Healing waits for those who give and receive love.

15

The Inner You

A recent documentary was presented by several psychiatrists who believe the stem of the brain may hold answers to some people's mental and emotional problems. The body's production of certain hormones and chemicals creates desirable effects.

In one experiment, a patient who suffered from chronic depression every winter was told to sit in front of a bright light for several hours each morning. After a period of time, the young woman's mental attitude improved considerably. The psychologists concluded that quite possibly the light, acting on a specific gland, caused the production of a hormone that "somehow" triggered a brighter attitude.

In my opinion, the *principle*, not the hormone, was the primary factor in the attitude change the woman experienced. I use that same principle all the time. God is the One who first introduced it.

The woman suffered basically from *undisciplined thoughts*. The light was a point of contact to hold her attention, thereby disciplining her mind until she got her thoughts under control for the day. In the experiment, she sat for several hours first thing each morning in a situation she had been told would possibly help her.

Let us take this same principle into the realm of the Holy Spirit. *Runaway thoughts are the primary problem in any mental or emotional disorder.* In spite of a person's physical condition, it is possible to discipline thoughts and thereby maintain a good mental attitude. This is precisely why God introduced the principle of *thought focus* in Isaiah 26:3: "Thou [the Lord] wilt keep him in perfect peace, whose mind is stayed [concentrated] on thee: because he trusteth in thee."

What am I saying? Is it all simply *mind control?* Not at all. I am saying, "Why sit in front of a light, or any other focusing object, when you can look directly to God, do what He says, and receive the benefits of the *workable principle*—plus receive the added help of the Holy Spirit of God himself?"

In addition to using God's sound principle and having the help of His Spirit, you can get help anywhere you happen to be. We cannot always drag around a four-foot light everywhere we go. But we can hide the Word of God in our heart. The moment our mind begins to lose control, we can grab onto a living promise from our Father and put the reins on our thoughts until they have quieted down.

God's ways work best! He has a plan for our every need. The greatest weakness in modern psychology is the overall thrust to find physical solutions to the problems of people who are made up of spirit, mind, and body. No person, school of thinking, or professional service fully addresses the problems of human beings unless spirit, mind, and body—all three—are recognized.

This is why the words of God are invaluable to the overall welfare of human beings. He has acknowledged and taken into account our total make-up. When He gives a word of instruction, we can be sure it is inclusive of all our needs and a principle that is as dependable as the eternal life-cycle.

Many times panic has hit my mind, especially when in the grips of emotional distress. Like the woman in the experiment, at those times I went straight for the Light! I praised Him, sang psalms of worship, and refreshed and renewed my mind with the eternal truths of God's unfailing Word. As a result, I never fell apart. Eventually I overcame the panic altogether. Even the slightest hint of panic now (especially when I am too tired) sends me straight to that Eternal Light. He always calms my thoughts with His great thoughts of peace. I settle down, and the fear passes.

I wrote a book on the nature of light. In one chapter, I discussed the unlimited ability of laser light to communicate. Theoretically, it is possible for one laser beam to hold every television program on the earth at one time.

The Bible says God *is* light. This means He has unlimited capacity to see the minutest detail in every one of our lives at the same time. Neither you not I could come up with anything too difficult for Him. He would already have a prepared solution.

I doubt that I have the attention of any real skeptics at this point. In case I do, bravo! Keep reading. But my prescription is never going to vary. After trying everything man has to offer, I came upon the Counselor who has all the answers. I have proved Him now for many years, and He is more than I had been told He was.

Sometimes I have been afraid. A few times I have even wanted to give up. I have floundered and yelled out for help. But in spite of the old thought patterns that tried to creep back in, I have continued taking my daily prescription of God's Word and slowly but surely come back into a life of stable emotions.

THE HELPER'S VOICE

I have learned to discipline my thoughts and recognize unprofitable conversation. I have achieved good mental and emotional health, but I did not do it alone. I had a tremendous Helper. His Name is the Holy Spirit of God.

This is our final prescription in renovating our thought processes. I take our counsel from Ephesians 4:30: "And grieve not [distress, offend] the holy Spirit of God, whereby ye are sealed [secured] unto the day of redemption [final deliverance]."

The Holy Spirit secures you for the day of deliverance. Do you truly want permanent help in your emotional life? Do you mean business? Have you decided to find a new way of thinking at all cost? If so, then you need to become acquainted with the Holy Spirit. You need to learn to recognize His voice and respect His presence. You need to learn His way of doing things.

Whatever your problems—fear, stress, anxiety, worry, depression, phobias, habits, perversions—God has sent His very own Spirit to work with you and guide you out of every situation and into the truth about your life.

Jesus said in John 14:26: "But the Comforter, which is the Holy Ghost, whom the Father will send in my name, he shall teach you all things...."

Your greatest comfort is the Holy Spirit. He comes for the express purpose of clearing your mind and drawing you closer to God. Many people live under heavy depression, fear, and anxiety because the devil has misquoted God's Word to them, pointing out failures and worthlessness. But when you know the Holy Spirit's voice, you will see that all such condemnation comes from Satan to discourage you. God clearly assures us that He sent Jesus into the world not to condemn the world "but that the world through him might be saved" (John 3:17).

Feeling like a louse has no redemptive value in it. Knowing what *causes* a person to become a louse is the way to avoid being one. For years I thought God was the one sending me depression and exaggerated fears. I thought He used these things to keep me spiritually alert and in line.

That makes about as much sense as burning your child with a match every day to teach him you are his loving parent!

When the Holy Spirit, also called the Spirit of Truth, speaks to you, He may point out a sin, a weakness, or an erroneous thought pattern in your life. But He always does it in such a way as to guide you in a better direction.

189

For example, let's say you are depressed because you feel you have failed God or some person near to you. You may have, in fact, failed one or both of them. The natural approach is to blame the circumstances. The devil's approach is to *condemn yourself.* The Holy Spirit's approach is to point out what *God's Word* says about it then show you a better way than the other two options.

The Holy Spirit never convicts you of your mistakes without showing you a way out and giving you hope to try again.

Ephesians 4:30 warns against grieving the Holy Spirit by listening to yourself or the devil. If you do, sooner or later you will give up. Do you realize that every time you give up, you agree with the devil? God's Spirit is here to help you get up and keep going forward.

But some of you have given up on happiness. You have thought it was useless to try any longer. As far as you know, you have been alone in your struggle, and you are weary.

Well, you don't have to fight the battles of life alone any longer. The same Spirit who created this beautiful earth out of a dark, unproductive state is here to recreate a new way of thinking in *your* dark, unproductive emotional state.

Let me ask you again: How far are you willing to go in order to change? All the way? No turning back? Through the years, I have found that many people will start on the journey to sound thinking, but few will continue to the finish line. The casualty list is great. Many hurting people come looking for a quick fix. When they don't get it, they move back into their old miserable routine and wonder why God helps everybody but them.

A woman came to Paul and I one evening in great distress. For the next few months we worked with her. Step by step, we carefully guided the woman into a new way of thinking. Each week her mental process got a little more renovation. The old, gray veil of depression began to fade from her eyes. She was coming closer and closer to stability when suddenly she stopped the renewal program and stayed home. Now she only calls us when she is desperate.

You see, what this woman and many other casualties do not realize is that good emotional health is not a six-month, self-improvement course. It is a new way of living.

You cannot just learn what to do, you must do it. You cannot just do it for a season, you must live that new way *forever*.

FINDING INNER PEACE

My husband and I visited a woman who has been in the process of recovering from a mental breakdown for over a year. We begged her to come to our center on a regular basis, but she did not find it possible. Instead, she left the country and spent several months in Europe. When she returned, we asked her how she enjoyed her trip.

"When you are miserable inside, no place is interesting," she responded.

I say "amen" to that. How well I know. Inner distress is never left at home. It goes everywhere you go despite your socio-economical level. Inner distress makes itself at home on Persian carpets as surely as it moves into one-room apartments.

Happiness, sound thinking, and stable emotions simply do not depend on natural circumstances. Inner peace is a condition of your spirit. This is why it is imperative that you become friends with God through His Holy Spirit.

Do you remember Rick, the young man I had mentioned in the introduction who had fallen apart emotionally? His body played games with his mind; his mind played games with his spirit; and his spirit played games with his answer.

The principles I have established in these chapters are guideposts in the right direction for such a person. There is no quick solution once you have come apart on the inside.

The pattern for renewed living applies to the healthy as well as the sick. Prevention is always better medicine than remedies.

If you have never fallen apart, thank God and put these laws of health into practice beginning today. If your body, mind, and spirit have become disjointed and seem to have become enemies with each other, you can end the battle by adopting these laws of health. If you will ever be emotionally stable, the "inner you"—that spirit person you are—must have the cooperation of your body and mind in all you do. You cannot lie in bed all day and hope to fill your mind with courage. You cannot constantly fill your emotions with wild thoughts and hope to correct your unrenewed mind by osmosis.

Health is not automatic. It requires the cooperation of body, mind, and spirit. You are a three-part composition. Each part of your unique make-up must be acknowledged if you want every part of you to be healthy.

My advice to Rick was to adopt the program by which I live every day:

1. **Get a job.** Obligate your body to produce. Bodies were designed to perform not petrify. Reasonable work is a must for the body as long as we live.

2. **Discipline your mind to go along with your obligations.** Do not allow fears, anxieties, or phantom threats to hinder your physical production. A mind can be taught. Once your mind sees that your body is actually able to take the stress, it will begin to comply with the regulations.

3. **Get back into fellowship with God and other believers.** Great strength can be gained through corporate worship and ministry. The Holy Spirit brings special grace where people unite together around the presence of God. Never mind those foolish thoughts that say you will choke, have a heart attack, or faint.

You are an eternal spirit. Nothing natural can ever destroy the real you. Strengthen the inner person you are. Let your spirit be the voice of authority over your mind and body. Under the direction of God's Holy Spirit, rise up, be strong, and do those things fear has been telling you are impossible.

YOUR ETERNAL LOVER

Have you ever been in love? The spiritual and emotional oneness was glorious, wasn't it? The sky was three shades bluer, rain felt like drops of vitality, and you looked younger. Everywhere you went, you took the glow of your lover's presence whether or not he or she was with you in person. You didn't even want to wash the hand he held. Depression would have suffocated in all that honey if it had attempted to settle in your mind! You had joined your heart with the perfect match. At least it seemed so at the moment.

But, as we all know, nothing natural is without its blights and blemishes. Many people end up disappointed and disappointing others. Emotions get wounded in the struggle, and roses don't revive our inner feelings.

You do have a Lover who will *never* disappoint you. He is the eternal Lover of your soul, and He has sent His Spirit here to build an eternal relationship with you. He cares about what you think, and He cares about how you feel. He enjoys listening to you talk. The sound of your voice is heavenly music when it is directed to Him. You are invited to call Him anytime, and He longs for the same invitation from you.

Nothing on this earth will ever satisfy your deepest longings and give you the peace of mind you desire like a close relationship with God—close, personal, and constant. You are, after all, first and last, spirit. You are spirit; you live in a body; and you possess a mind.

Troubles may have caused natural happiness to divorce you, but God's Spirit is here to join with your spirit in a joyous relationship independent of anything and anybody. God says that if we want to have peace of mind, we must be careful to maintain our spiritual union with Him.

Have you ever been in love? Weren't you full and bursting with desire?

Then pray this prayer with me:

> "Father, in the Name of Jesus, I surrender. I give up! I have tried everything I know, but nothing seems to work. Now I am coming to You. I confess my own failures, and I ask You to forgive me. I have been guilty of blaming other people for my misery, but now I forgive them. Father, *I ask You to fill me with Your Holy Spirit.* Rebuild my mind, my thoughts, and my inner self, and let me experience once again the joy of being alive!"

God's Word contains various truths that we need in order to be sane, balanced, and sociable human beings. There is no one answer to restoring your mind or emotions. But there is one *Book* that contains all answers to the five billion questions that arise in the hearts of men, women, and children each day.

Take the Bible—take the Spirit—take your eyes off your misery and start looking for the answers in the best place with the greatest Person.

I have stated many principles in this book. Each one of them has been laboratory-tested by me personally. They are eternal concepts that will work for any person willing to live by them every day for as long as he or she needs them. It is a new way of life that will never wash out from under any person.

Each morning, as you wake up and stretch, point your arms in the direction of the Lover of your soul. Ask Him to fill you with His Spirit for that day. Give your thoughts to God. Ask Him to take control of your life. Then get out of bed, get dressed, and start living!

In our next and final chapter, I want to talk to you about taking the right approach to the rest of your life.

16

Taking the Right Approach to the Rest of Your Life

Invasion is a mind set coined at least two hundred years ago on the fires of the great revivals. "Storming the gates of heaven" became the watch word of past century prayer warriors.

But when you stop to examine the word and act of invasion, you find that it actually implies behavior that is unacceptable in the sacred realm where prayers are heard and answered. According to Webster, invasion means "hostile entrance, infringement, violation."

The invasion mentality does not apply to the kingdom of heaven. The only place we find it acceptable is in the realm of sin. Believers have a right to invade the territories and people held captive by Satan. We are in fact commanded to set the captives free.

But worship and reverence and sober respect for God is the only way to come into the realm of the Spirit and hope to be heard. Angry, demanding, ill-considered, selfish invasion into the presence of God accomplishes little. Man can be intimidated, but God cannot. I have found that threats only tend to stir up God's anger. I even believe hostile attitudes provoke a certain stubbornness in God that says, "We'll see about that."

On the other hand, requests and supplications brought before God that have been meditated upon and well-thought out, receive a warm welcome. And if you add humility and a repentant attitude, you are certain to be heard.

There is a word in theology—*anthropomorphism*— which means the man-qualities of God. Not that God is part man, but we are created in the image of God. We do not possess all the power abilities of God, but we do possess the pattern of His spiritual and emotional character. We and God have some features in common. Invasive behavior that turns us off also offends God. So far as record shows, there has been only one invasion of heaven. That was Satan, and even it came as no surprise. Before there was ever an angel to rebel, God had already dealt with the possibility of sin and declared himself the Winner.

God can be approached, but He will never again be invaded. He plans a few dramatic invasions of His own as the end of human history draws to a close, but His gates have been invaded for the first and last time.

Anyone hoping to successfully reach God needs to lay aside all natural weapons—such as anger toward God. "I never get a fair break"; or spite—"I'll never set foot in church again"; or manipulation—"I'll do this,

God, if You'll do this"; or presumption—"God understands my sins." He needs to step back and take another look at what works.

A planeload of people made a long flight and were coming in for a landing when the pilot missed the approach. He invaded the runway, the plane caught fire and many people died. Invading heaven with childish behavior or erroneous presumption causes numerous casualties among our prayer requests. Sometimes everything we thought should be ours, dies.

USING THE RIGHT APPROACH

God began to declare the need for the right approach into His presence in the Garden of Eden. The moment sin entered the human scene, man was no longer welcome to approach God on the direct basis he had formerly enjoyed.

Before Adam sinned, he was perfect—sinless. He had no problem being in the direct presence of the Holy God. After Adam sinned, however, man would never again be sinless in the sense that God is sinless. By the shed blood, man could have his sins removed, forgotten, and paid for—but his unmediated approach to God was lost forever. Because of sin, man would forever have to approach God through a Mediator.

I know many well-meaning Christians have talked about jumping up in God's big lap and calling Him "Daddy," and this does not offend God—He is our Father. He desires closeness and fellowship with us. But He also understands that we are talking about things we do not comprehend. To jump up in God's lap would be like jumping into the lap of the Milky Way—or putting your arms around the sun and giving it a great big hug.

God can be reached. He can be touched. But touching Him is on a much higher and even more satisfying plane than a physical embrace. Spiritual communion has an ecstasy, a wonder, a glory that nothing we have experienced in flesh can fully describe. But this kind of communion with God happens only for those who have stopped trying to make God a mere mortal. Deep communion with God happens for those who have learned how to enter into the realm of the spirit and take the right approach before a God so large He calls earth His footstool. Believers do not have to be afraid of God. Yet it helps to understand just how big He is.

We live in a day when reverence for sacred things is viewed with skepticism. But skeptics have no approach to God. "For he that comes to God must believe that He is..." Paul said. Until he becomes willing to lay down his skepticism and seek God humbly, a skeptic will keep missing the runway.

The notion that whatever we believe will somehow "hit upon God" and succeed is a notion as unfounded and foolish as it is popular. Nothing about God has ever suggested that just any idea can land safely at His airport, regardless the approach it takes. Every endeavor in life has a proper (and improper) approach. This fact began to be evidenced thousands of years ago when God first began to interact with a man called Abraham and his descendants. What God taught the human race through these people was the right approach to life. He taught them how to live as friends with time.

THE RIGHT APPROACH TO A NEW DAY

Take for example the Jewish way of counting time. Whereas, most of the world calls a day from midnight to midnight, the Jewish day is counted from sunset to sunset. When you stop to think about it, it makes sense. The sun is setting, the busyness of life is settling down, you are hungry and want to go home. With the family together, you refresh your body with food, your relationships with conversation, and you then settle down to relax and draw your soul aside from the world. It is a perfect time to commune with God, in light of tomorrow's challenges. King David often meditated upon God after he had retired to bed. It was preparation for the daylight hours ahead of him.

Today, television robs much of our time for meditation, when we could relax on the sofa or in bed, and converse with God about our life and plans. Occupied by media programming, we forget that life is precious. Each new day is a gift from God. He wants us to approach it with sober respect and spiritual direction. This is why He gives us the quiet "evening approach" to the busyness of daylight hours.

A day without "evening refreshment" and spiritual reflection is plunged into on the wings of numerous blunders and mistakes. "How did I make that mistake in judgment?" we ask. Because we did not bother with the right approach. We did not get the "God view." We made no preparation—we just "invaded" the daylight hours on blind instinct. The beginning of a new day should start the evening before. It is the best time to focus on what lies ahead.

THE RIGHT APPROACH TO A NEW WEEK

As with the gift of each new day, so it is with each new week. "Work shall be done for six days, but the seventh is the Sabbath of rest, holy to the Lord." Stop and think about all the things that can transpire in one week's time. Marriages take place that set people's life on a course where new lives will be brought into this world for good or evil, forever. Souls go out into eternity—thousands of souls each week—sealing their destiny forever. Nations transact agreements that affect the lives of billions of people every week. Fortunes are made and fortunes are lost, men achieve and men fail; dreams are birthed and dreams die—all in one week's time.

Surely we need the right approach to such a life-shaping frame of days. God knew this, and in order to help prevent our crashing on the runway, He instituted the Sabbath day as a time of spiritual and mental refreshment for the week ahead.

On the Roman Calendar, the days of the week have names—Monday, Tuesday, Wednesday and so forth. In Hebrew, only one day of the week has a name—Sabbath. Every other day of the week is merely first, second, third, and so on, until the seventh comes and that is highlighted as Sabbath.

Sabbath is the "right approach" day that makes the week succeed. If worship and communion with God are carefully observed, our days and weeks go right. If Sabbath is ignored, mistakes and disasters follow. God's original death penalty for failing to observe a Sabbath of refreshing with Him was a graphic example of what happens to a life that ignores God. Sooner or later all its plan's die. Regular worship with other believers is the right approach to a new week.

The right approach to each new day—

the right approach to each new week—

then comes the right approach to each new month. If one day is noteworthy, and one week can be earth shaking, imagine the magnitude of what transpires between the heavens and earth in one whole month's time.

THE RIGHT APPROACH FOR THE NEW MONTH

In ancient Israel, the first day of each month was sanctified and set apart from all other days. At the sighting of the new moon by two reliable witnesses, the priests would issue the declaration, "It is sanctified."

According to ancient custom, once the new moon was declared, a telegraph system of fires were set across the Arabian desert that reached from Jerusalem to Babylon in only minutes, and Jews everywhere were called to a time of reflection and celebration of the Rosh Hodesh (New Month). Special sacrifices were offered, along with the blowing of trumpets and the new month was dedicated to God. A new month where God is not consulted is a month without a compass.

Every one of us owns numerous calendars. They are in our homes, at our office, and in our billfolds. We even have appointment books where we write out our schedule for the month. But what about God? Have we written God into our calendar for the month? Was He consulted regarding our scheduling? Have we prayed over those thirty or so wonderful days of opportunities from Him, asking God to bless, guide and direct?

The right approach to a day, leads to—
the right approach to a week, that leads to—
the right approach to a month, that leads to—
the right approach to a year, which leads to—
a life in focus.

A balanced, sound view of life is the result of approaching the time given us under the direction of God.

THE NEW YEAR

A unique thing happened in ancient Israel concerning the new year and the calendar. It is unmistakable evidence of the whole point of this chapter on how to get the right approach to life. Israel actually has two calendars—one civil, one religious.

The civil or agricultural New Year was always observed by Israel after the harvest season was over (September-October). Yet, after God delivered them from slavery in Egypt, Moses appointed Nisan (March-April) as Israel's religious New Year. This tells us that so long as time lasts, the spiritual person has two calendars. One is his natural responsibilities, the other is his spiritual appointments and assignments with God.

A person with only a natural calendar is out of step with reality. His perspective is distorted. He is operating at only half his potential. Without the spiritual approach to life, sooner or later our natural calendar will come crashing down around us, and all our plans will evaporate into yesterdays. Each new day, each new week, each new month, each new year, are gifts of time from God that will reach their maximum fulfillment only as we make time to take the spiritual approach to life.

The spiritual perspective is the right approach to the rest of your life. It is the only approach that guarantees true success.

To prove my point, I invite you to turn now to the Epilogue for one of the greatest stories of all time. It is a true life venture that includes all the elements of the mind and emotion we have discussed in this book. I want you to follow in the footsteps of a mind set on a goal, and I want you to observe how much a person's success depends on his or her attitude. I call this true event from history, "The Silk Road." Not only is "The Silk Road" true, but it is every person's journey with fear and courage as he seeks to carry out his mission in life. I wanted to include this particular story in this book as evidence of just how powerful (or weak) a mind can be, and how far reaching its effects. It stands as a monument to all who question the power of a determined heart.

Epilogue

The Silk Road

One of the most fascinating journals from the library of ancient history was written by a young Venetian merchant in the late 1200s. At a time when travel was much more dangerous than it is today, Marco Polo, along with his father and uncle, set out on a venture that lasted twenty-four years. It was a search for the rare treasures of China.

When the Polos left for China—with dreams of silks, spices and precious gems—men still thought the earth was flat. This meant that any serious traveler not only had to risk real life-threatening dangers from robbers and natural elements, but they also had to fight the phantoms of the mind. A traveler never knew when he would just come to the edge of his world and perhaps fall off.

In those days merchants also had to work in relays—one group would meet another and pass on its goods. Information traveled the same way. The sailors who brought the goods the last stage of the journey could tell nothing of the lands from which the treasures originally came. But for some merchants, the profits justified the risks. Being such a family, the Polos set out alone in search of the eastern treasures, on a path that came to be called "The Silk Road."

The Silk Road is an awesome journey in any generation. It offers both the greatest threats as well as the greatest rewards. Yet, in the realm of the Spirit, it is the only road where the treasures of truth travel.

Let me ask you a question: How much are you willing to pay for something you want? How much are you willing to endure to go all the way to the house of The Great Sovereign in order to discover His secret wealth? How much are you willing to sacrifice in order to bring back rare truths to other people?

Jesus said, "The kingdom of heaven is like a merchant seeking beautiful pearls, who, when he had found one pearl of great price, went and sold all that he had and bought it" (Matthew 13:45,46).

How far will a good merchant go in search of valuable merchandise? Let's take a look now at the trials three men endured along the Silk Road, and let us compare their response with others on the same journey, keeping in mind our own responses to fear and intimidating circumstances.

THE SILK ROAD

The first thing we need to know about the Silk Road is the fact that many start out on its journey only to turn back when the going gets sufficiently threatening. The only people who will go all the way are those who have a vision for their mission. A second-hand vision will not last. Traditional religious faith and long-held thought patterns are not sufficient to endure the mountains to be faced on the journey to something of value.

When Marco Polo set out for China with his father and uncle, there were actually two other men in their party. During the first visit of Marco's father with the Great Khan, he had told the emperor about western man's religion. Above all else, the Khan wanted to hear more about this. The Polos therefore requested two Dominican friars be sent with them to more clearly explain the Christian faith.

When the little party of five reached Turkey, however, their troubles started. To begin with, the road through Armenia was rough and narrow. Sometimes it became a single track across desert sands. Rivers and ledges cut into the sides of steep cliffs had to be crossed. One slip and deep gorges with dangerous rapids lay below. Added to the natural hazards, when the party met a band of armed men who told them there was fighting going on in Armenia, the friars refused to go another step. Turning instead toward the city of Jerusalem, the two potential evangelists took a path that would ensure their own safety.

Imagine how different China might have been for the past seven hundred years if the friars had set their hearts to tell the Great Khan about Jesus Christ at any cost? What if Kubla Khan had been converted to faith in Christ and his court had become a mission to the billions of Chinese who have lived and died since the thirteenth century? What a tremendous opportunity lay ahead for the two friars! If only they had looked beyond their natural circumstances to the spiritual door that lay open before them, how many lives might have been ushered into the everlasting kingdom. But without a vision they grew faint-hearted and went back to safety.

Only the three men with a vision kept going in the face of danger. Sometimes the Polos traveled on foot, sometimes on mules or camels. At night they often slept out under the stars. In the day they sweltered in the scorching heat of the Persian Gulf, only to approach another extreme where they shivered in the bitter cold of high mountains. Sometimes they were even attacked by bandits and had to take refuge within a walled city.

Allow me to tell you about one such attack the Polos encountered that teaches us another truth about a merchant's journey on the Silk Road. It is the secret to overcoming the "magic fog."

OVERCOMING THE "MAGIC FOG"

On the Polo's way down to the Port of Hormuz, they along with other merchants were attacked by bandits known to terrorize the region. You see, Satan divides a nation, or a city, or even a family into various regions. He then sets up his reputation over those regions. Some regions he marks off as too steeped in a false religion to be evangelized. Others he declares to be too intellectual. Some are considered too wealthy and advanced, some too poor. Whatever the reputation, it is designed to keep people on the Silk Road from carrying out their mission. Satan's desire is always to stop the flow of spiritual merchandise and the healing it will bring to the hearts and minds of its recipients.

In the case of the Polos, they were suddenly assaulted by bandits who were believed by locals to raise a "magic fog" when they attacked—which confused and frightened their victims. We know today that this "dry fog" was nothing more than fine dust particles stirred up by hot winds. But unless we are wise to the strategies of the enemy, he will pounce on us at some unsuspecting moment and cause the phantoms of our mind to defeat us. In the frenzy, the grief, the shock of the natural circumstances, we may lose sight of our good purpose and go back to our comfort zone.

The Word of God says, "Finally, my brethren, be strong in the Lord and in the power of His might. Put on the whole armor of God, that you may be able to stand against the wiles of the devil" (Ephesians 6:10,11). The word "wiles" is from the Greek *methodias* from which we get our English "method." It refers to all the various methods of "magic fog" Satan whips up around our lives to intimidate and cause us to give up.

Ask yourself, "Why do robbers attack their victims?" Is it not to steal, kill and destroy? (See John 10:10.) They come to get us off the Silk Road and stop the flow of spiritual treasures. They also like, as a bonus, to take what belongs to us.

A robber's method of attack is surprise; his motive is confusion. But his purpose is to blur our vision and stop our successful journey. Confusion is a bandit on the journey to the Emperor's Court. If you lose sight of why you're doing what you're doing, all life will drain out of what you're doing.

Do you know how Marco Polo and his party survived the deadly combination of mental phantoms and real dangers that suddenly came upon them? They took refuge in a walled city.

For the person who sees his attackers coming yet refuses to bow down and surrender his treasures, there is a place of refuge. God has not put us on a journey through life with no protection. "In the fear of the Lord there is strong confidence, and His children will have a place of refuge" (Proverbs 14:26).

Every living person comes under attack from time to time. Doing the will of God does not eliminate us from enemy invasion. The greatest apostle to ever travel the Silk Road said of his journey, "...Five times I received forty stripes minus one. Three times I was beaten with rods; once I was stoned; three times I was shipwrecked; a night and a day I have been in the deep; in journeys often, in perils of waters, in perils of robbers, in perils of my own countrymen, in perils of the Gentiles, in perils in the city, in perils in the wilderness, in perils in the sea, in perils among false brethren; in weariness and toil, in sleeplessness often, in hunger and thirst, in fastings often, in cold and nakedness" (2 Corinthians 11:24-27 NKJV).

At the same time Paul was encountering the robbers who wanted to stop the spread of his merchandise, it is recorded of the other apostles that when, "...They had called the apostles and beaten them, they commanded that they should not speak in the name of Jesus.... And they [disciples] departed from the presence of the council, rejoicing that they were counted worthy to suffer shame for His [Jesus'] name" (Acts 5:40,41).

Rejoicing in God in the face of trial was not a shallow applause for the apostles. In the midst of their rejoicing these men knew that they would continue to face this kind of opposition so long as they remained in the business of being God's merchants. Instead of a shallow pep rally, their rejoicing was in reality a deadly attack against an enemy who cannot bear to hear God being worshipped. In their rejoicing, the apostles were actually gearing up for the next encounter by taking the offensive.

One would think that after being brutalized or scandalized for the sake of a vision, God would pick up His followers and hide them in a safe place for a long recovery. But the truth is, an attack of the enemy often precedes the most grueling experiences we have yet to encounter. Look at what happened next to the Polos, and you will see what I mean.

Cautiously saying good-bye to a brief respite in the walled city, Marco Polo's team set out, of all places, against the naked desert! And just when we expected God to say, "You can go back home now where it's safe," we also enter into a spiritual drought where, from all appearance, heaven has shut down. At the very moment when we are convinced that we are on our last breath and cannot possibly go one step farther, God points to a great and impossible mountain that He wants us to conquer!

"Why me, Lord? Don't you know I almost lost my life back there?"

"I know," God answers. "Trust me."

Feebly we lift our hands and join in rejoicing with the apostles, and proof of God's faithfulness begins to work its way into our own private experience with the Master Merchant.

We have studied the maps, we've talked about "The Road," but now we are called to experience it. We conquered the mountain only to come to the desert. Is there no end to the testing? This is precisely what the Polos faced for several months following their attack by the "magic fog." First the desert, then the mountains, until finally the determined merchants reached a grim and forbidding place where there was no life at all, except for occasional water holes that lay more than a day's march apart. Marco Polo wrote of this place: "It is a well-known fact that this desert is the abode of evil spirits which lure travelers to their destruction. Losing the right path, and not knowing how to get back to it, they perish miserably of hunger." [1]

THE ULTIMATE TESTING

The desert abode of evil spirits was the mountain Jesus faced immediately following His baptism with water and the Spirit, when His mission as the Lamb of God was made public.

Somehow we Christians have always missed the point that once you declare your mission to travel the Silk Road in search of eternal treasures, Satan sets up a strategy to defeat you. With Jesus he began by challenging Him to satisfy His flesh and forget about the Spirit. Natural temptations are the primary attacks against a new believer, or a new commitment. From flesh Satan went next to Jesus' mind and encouraged Him to do something "eye catching" to prove Himself. When natural attacks no longer work, Satan moves to a second level of strategy involving the pride and vanity of the imagination—we catch a vision of all we could become. When that does not work, as it didn't work with Jesus, Satan offered Jesus the ultimate desire—power over people.

Power over people is perhaps the most treacherous part of a merchant's journey on the Silk Road. It was a time Jesus had to face alone without one word of encouragement. No friends—not even family. No one was there but Jesus, the temptation, and the "right path" out of the grim, forbidding mountain.

Without doubt it must have been the most electrifying encounter known in history—the Prince of Life and the Prince of Death, locked eye to eye in the ultimate temptation. It was a moment when the sum total of the human race hung in the balance between two merchants. And the choice was up to Jesus. Demons must have panted restlessly as they licked their fingers for the souls of men. Angels must have held their breath without even so much as the blinking of an eye—as they watched the stony glare of the two men on the mountain-side experience of the Silk Road.

A rumbling, a shaking, little pebbles began to trickle down from the dusty slopes. A quaking, a birthing, a dividing of the pelvic bones and the sound came shattering through the very gut of the boulders, "IT IS WRITTEN!!" The right path through the "abode of evil" is the Word of God. Jesus took it. And Jesus emerged from the barren wilderness pure, empowered, and equipped to go all the way. The Son of God had passed the ultimate testing for every merchant in search of lasting wealth. He proved once and for all, that God's Word will deliver from the gravest and most deceiving strategies of the devil—that God's Word is the "right path" to the watering holes of life where our soul finds refreshment—and that God's Word is the only dependable compass by which to attempt our life's journey. But beyond the safety factors provided in God's Word, Jesus showed us that nothing this world offers can compare with the treasures we will discover on the grueling but rewarding Silk Road that leads to the presence of the Sovereign God.

Do you have any idea what Marco Polo found once he had arrived at the capital of the Great Emperor of China? He found every inch of his arduous journey luxuriously rewarded. The king lived in a wonderful city with beautiful straight roads, high walls with twelve gates and many towers, and each gate was guarded by a thousand soldiers.

The Khan's palace stood high on a marble platform, and the walls inside were decorated in gold and fine paintings. His banqueting hall could serve six thousand guests at one time. It was a kingdom with such splendor that Marco Polo remained in the presence of the king for many years. It was a time when he was able to accumulate great personal wealth, knowledge and skill that would never have been available in the comfort of Venice.

It takes time in the presence of God to have the truth and wisdom of the Scriptures opened to our understanding. Meeting God comes at the moment of the new birth—when we come alive spiritually. But we must go into the presence of the King and wait for Him to bring out His various treasure boxes, if we will go away with His wealth. The treasure boxes of God are His words. As we read the Scriptures, we are looking at boxes that contain the most precious of all valuables. Life, hope, healing is in each word from God. But those boxes have to be opened to our understanding—and that takes patient meditation before the King.

Through the years in the Great Kahn's court, Marco Polo gained vast wealth from his royal treasury. He also developed a respect and genuine love for the king. Added to his affection there also developed the faithful heart of a true servant to the great sovereign.

Ultimately, however, Marco Polo faced what every person who goes into the presence of God must face. It was the same reality the three lepers faced in the day of famine in Israel when they discovered food. "It is not good that we hold our peace," they said to each other. "We must go back and tell the others."

Marco Polo—older, wiser, richer—along with his father and uncle, left the courts of the king's palace and set out once again on the Silk Road, where they would go back and deliver the riches they had acquired to those waiting to purchase. Were the merchants well received when they finally arrived back in Venice? Hardly. Most people did not even recognize them. Their years spent apart with the great king had brought about considerable change. Their struggles on the Silk Road had wearied their bodies as well as their clothes. Their appearance actually caused the people to start laughing at them.

Time in the presence of God always changes our appearance in the eyes of the world. Try as we may, a Truth-soaked, Word-soaked, God-soaked person is an offense to the world. Three shabbily dressed men stood amidst the laughter of the freshly groomed Venetians. But it was a laughter that was soon to fall on the scorners' heads like pounding rocks. Weary but standing, the three Polos pulled back their tired coats to expose the linings. Taking the glistening point of a sharp travelers' knife, like skillful surgeons they gave one sharp slit and pouring out like sparkling waters came handfuls of priceless treasures—pearls, rubies and diamonds. It was the very treasures for which the hearts of the Venetians longed.

The Bible says the Gospel—the good news of God, the Word— is a traveler making a tour of the whole earth. He rides in the merchant's bag of every believer. And He brings great profit to those who tell and those who hear. "...The word of the truth of the gospel, which has come to you, as it has in all the world, and is bringing forth fruit..." (Colossians 1:5,6). The longings of the heart, the needs of the mind and emotion, will ultimately find their greatest satisfaction in God—His Word and His work.

The question remains, who will pay the price to travel the Silk Road, that the treasures of God may become real to them? Who will take the risks required of a good merchant to help someone else discover the answers to his or her questions about life?

Perhaps you are another Marco Polo. As you have read this story, you may have said, "I'm willing to take the risks to go in search of the Great King, and to stay in His presence until my soul has been restored, and I have something of value to bring to the people who are hungry for God and God's answers. If so, may I suggest the following qualifications of a good merchant?

1. Get a vision.
2. Don't allow the strategies of the enemy to intimidate you.
3. Stay on the "right path" by using the Word of God.
4. Learn to serve the King.
5. Go out and share what you have discovered with others.

The Silk Road is not easy journey, but it is exceedingly rewarding and it's treasures are certain as well as eternal.

<u>Notes</u>
1. Marco Polo. *A Description of the World.*

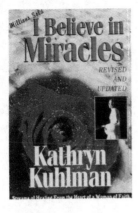

The 90's: Decade of the Apocalypse
Steve Terrell

As of December 31, 1992, the member nations of the European Common Market have dissolved all existing trade barriers between each other. They seek to establish their own trans-national currency system. They will elect their own president.

If you think this is all coincidence, read this startling book.

ISBN 0-88270-707-8 • Trade/188 pp.
$ 6.95

Europe After Democracy
Arthur H. Brown

Well known throughout Canada as a pastor, conference speaker, and gospel music artist for three decades, Arthur H. Brown has finally published his much sought-after expertise on the book of Revelation. No serious student of eschatology can pass up this most well-organized, detailed, and insightful study of Revelation on the market today.

ISBN 0-88270-709-4 • 6x9/385 pp.
$9.95

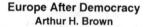

**Europe
After
Democracy**

New Release

Life in the Millennium
Mona Johnian

The Church has looked to it with joyful anticipation since the moment the Lord ascended into Glory, but what does the millennium *mean*, and what will it be like? Learn from one of the most sought-after teachers in the northeast as she simply and clearly illuminates the glory that is in store for the people of God!

ISBN 0-88270-705-1 • Trade/195 pp.
$ 7.95